A Winter in the Middle of Two Seas

Real Stories from Bahrain

Ronald W. Kenyon

CreateSpace

2013

The author has striven for accuracy and has endeavored to verify all factual information. All the opinions expressed herein are the author's, and he alone bears the responsibility for any errors in the text.

Map of Bahrain copyright © WordTravels.com. Reproduced by permission of the copyright holder.

This book is available at quantity discounts for bulk purchase. For information, please email the author at rwkenyon@gmail.com.

Copyright © 2013, 2016 Ronald W. Kenyon
All rights reserved

ISBN-13: 978-1478388661
ISBN-10: 1478388668

This book is dedicated to the people of Bahrain in the earnest hope that they may, with God's grace, achieve everlasting harmony.

Table of Contents

A Winter in the Middle of Two Seas 11

Looking for Dilmun…and the Seef Mall 19

"Are You Going to Saudi Arabia?" 27

Schadenfreude 41

Sunnis, Shias, Christians and Jews 47

Shopping 59

Kenyon's Law 71

Dilmun and Ashura 77

Thobes, Bishts, Uniforms and Shirts 89

Qatar 97

The Wrap-up 109

The Truth about Bahrain 121

Index 135

About the Author 141

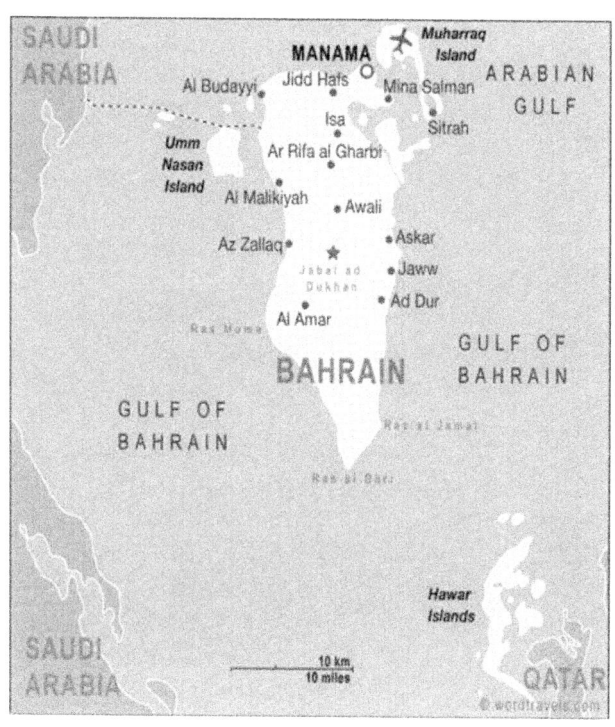

A Winter in the Middle of Two Seas

Bahrain. What is it? Where is it? Why are you going there? Those were some of the questions I was asked by my friends before my scheduled departure in late 2010.

What I discovered is that most people don't know much of anything about Bahrain. Some people confuse or conflate Bahrain with the nearby United Arab Emirates, especially Dubai, which many people have heard of, either because the world's highest building, Burj Khalifa, is located there or because of its spectacular real estate crash when apartments often lost as much as two-thirds of their value overnight. Others knew about Dubai because of its location as a stopover on flights between Europe and Asia and its well-stocked duty-free stores. But Bahrain isn't Dubai.

President Franklin D. Roosevelt did, in fact, know what Bahrain was and where it was. In a conversation with Mrs. Roosevelt[1] at the presidential retreat at Hyde Park, NY, on August 8, 1939, shortly before the arrival of a Bahraini emissary, President Roosevelt told her, "I have always known [Bahrain] because, you see, I collect stamps." [2] I also discovered that more of my British friends knew about Bahrain than my American friends, mainly because, under a series of treaties in the 19th century, Bahrain became a British protectorate.

---

[1] The American Presidency Project. Franklin D. Roosevelt. Excerpts from the Press Conference in Hyde Park, NY, August 8, 1939.

[2] On May 15, 1947, Monaco issued a postage stamp depicting President Roosevelt with his stamp collection.

The archipelago was under British domination from 1820 until 1971 although there were sporadic uprisings and movements for sovereignty. Bahrain gained its independence on August 15, 1971. Even today, commercial and government ties with Britain remain strong.

So, what is Bahrain? It is an archipelago of 33 islands, the largest of which is named, logically, Bahrain. Its area covers an extent of 765 square kilometers or 295 square miles, which makes it the 190th largest country in the world. Bahrain Island is 55 km (34 mi) long by 18 km (11 mi) wide. Bahrain's population in 2012 was 1,234,571, including 666,172 expatriates from countries all over the world, but mostly from Southwest Asia.

Bahrain has a high adult literacy rate—94.6 percent—a Gross Domestic Product of around $27,000 per capita per annum (the equivalent figure for the United States is $48,000), and the government provides free education and healthcare for its citizens.

And where is Bahrain? It is located near the western shore of a body of water that goes by three different names depending on who you are or where you are. Arabs call it the "Arabian Gulf" because—along with predominantly Arab Bahrain—the Arab nations of Kuwait, Iraq, Saudi Arabia, Qatar, the United Arab Emirates and Oman lie along its shores. Americans and Iranians tend to call this body of water the "Persian Gulf," even though Persia no longer exists; the name was officially replaced by

"Iran" in 1935. Nobody calls it the Iranian Gulf. British media and expatriates just call it "the Gulf." I opted for British usage in this book.

Saudi Arabia lies to the west and is connected to Bahrain via the King Fahd Causeway, 25 kilometers (16 miles) long, officially opened to traffic on November 25, 1986. The causeway is named for the late king of Saudi Arabia, which financed the $800 million project. Currently some 25,000 vehicles cross the causeway each day.

Qatar lies to the southeast across the Gulf of Bahrain. The Qatar-Bahrain Friendship Bridge is projected to link the two nations as the longest bridge in the world.

The word "Bahrain" means "two seas" in Arabic. Although the archipelago lies in the middle of the Gulf, the term refers to fresh-water springs that once bubbled up in the shallow salt water offshore. It is claimed that this combination of fresh and salt water imparted a particular luster to the pearls that were harvested by the Bahrainis from antiquity and were responsible for the early renown and prosperity of the island.

The Al Khalifa family, who rule Bahrain today, arrived on the islands in the 18th century to deal in oysters and pearls. Historians describe the heyday of the pearl trade in Bahrain as something akin to court life in Renaissance Italy, with cosmopolitan ruling families comparable to the Medicis and Borgias.

Why did I go to Bahrain? I had been engaged to conduct training courses for young Bahrainis preparing for careers as aviation mechanics and engineers. These courses are provided as part of an employment and training program sponsored and financed by Tamkeen, a semi-autonomous agency of the Bahraini Government, budgeted at 4.8 million Bahraini dinars or $12.72 million.

The thinking behind this program seems to be that Bahrain, which is poor in natural resources—oil production is currently between 35,000 and 50,000 barrels per day—is rich in human resources. Currently the aviation sector is booming in the Gulf, and each nation on its shores boasts one or more national carriers. The venerable Gulf Air, founded in 1950, and newcomer Bahrain Air are based in the island nation, Qatar Airways proclaims itself the world's five-star airline, and the United Arab Emirates are the home of Etihad Airways, Emirates Airlines, Air Arabia and around three dozen charter, cargo and government fleets. All these aircraft need regular maintenance and repairs. The Bahraini authorities believe that their country can become the hub for aircraft servicing in the Gulf and consider aircraft maintenance an excellent vehicle for integrating young Bahrainis—particularly those from the Shia Muslim religious community—into society by offering them excellent training and guaranteed jobs.

I arrived in Bahrain on October 24, 2010, the day after Bahrain's parliamentary and municipal elections,[3] which have been held every four years starting in 2002.

I left Bahrain on the night of February 13, 2011, only a few hours before crowds of Shia activists demonstrated in the streets of Bahrain in what they called their "Day of Rage." Bahrain hasn't been the same since.

During those 112 days within what I choose to call the peaceful parentheses—that winter in the middle of two seas—I spent some of my spare time writing my personal observations about Bahrain in a series of letters, which I circulated to a group of friends. Those letters, revised and expanded in mid-2012, became the basis for the real stories of Bahrain recounted herein.

---

[3] Katzman, Kenneth. "Bahrain: Reform, Security, and U.S. Policy." Congressional Research Service, June 29, 2012.

Looking for Dilmun...and the Seef Mall

This was not going to be my first trip to Bahrain.

Thirty years ago, I was working in Saudi Arabia for an American company, also in the aviation sector. Like most American expatriates working in what we nicknamed "the Kingdom," the employees enjoyed not only good tax-free salaries, but excellent benefits including membership in the credit union, a dining hall with three subsidized meals a day, and a shuttle service connecting the various residences with the main office.

The company also had a recreation department that offered a program of activities to the employees and their dependents. From time to time the recreation department would organize trips on Thursdays and Fridays, the Saudi weekend. One of the most popular activities was a day-trip to the famous souk– the open-air market—in the town of Hofuf, the administrative center of the Eastern Province. Hofuf has been a trading center on the trans-Arabian caravan routes since time immemorial, and the souk covers a large area in the center of town. In fact, it is several adjacent markets including a gold souk and a ladies' souk that is off-limits to men.

On one occasion, the recreation department announced a week-end trip to Manama, the capital of Bahrain; I was one of the first to sign up. In those days, the causeway linking Saudi Arabia and Bahrain had not been built, so the prospect of a voyage on the Gulf, albeit a short one, and the discovery of another country, was especially appealing to me, a landlubber born and raised in hilly Appalachia a thousand miles from the sea.

On Thursday morning, we would board a dhow, the ancient Arabian seagoing vessel identified by its characteristic lateen sail. We would sightsee and spend the night at a hotel in Manama and return to our port of departure, Al Khobar, on Friday afternoon.

Every day I am reminded of that trip taken so long ago. Around my neck hangs a solid gold pendant that I bought in a jeweler's shop in Manama at the time. The pendant is an exact reproduction of a seal dating from the little-known Dilmun civilization, which flourished around 3,000 B.C. on Bahrain and in parts of the Arabian Peninsula ranging from Kuwait in the West to Abu Dhabi in the East.

As in present-day Japan, the seals—each one different—were used in ancient Dilmun to authenticate property or attest to a person's identity.

The seal reproduced on my pendant depicts two men using long straws to drink what archeologists believe to be a beverage made from fermented grain—the ancestor of today's beers and ales—out of a large amphora. Since the beverage was fermented inside the amphora, the straws would have been necessary to avoid ingesting the solid residue that collected at the bottom of the vessel, known to brewers as slops. The original seal, along with many others depicting anthropomorphic, zoömorphic or geometric symbols, is in the collection of the National Museum of Bahrain; the authorized reproductions were cast one at a time using the lost wax process.

The seal's design—known colloquially as the Beer Drinkers—is one of the most famous symbols of Bahrain's ancient past. Along with three other Dilmun seals, it is reproduced in large scale on the exterior of the National Bank of Bahrain building. The same seals are engraved on the reverse of a one-dinar banknote issued in 1998.

The Beer Drinkers seal is so famous that a stylized version was adopted as the corporate logo of the Tatton Brewery in Cheshire, England.

Sometimes I will show the gold pendant to people and tell them that it is a magic talisman that had transported me back to its home in Bahrain.

The first and definitive study of the Dilmun culture is Geoffrey Bibby's book, *Looking for Dilmun*, whose first edition was published in 1969, and which I first read at the time of my first visit to Bahrain. Bibby led the Danish Archeological Expedition to Bahrain, exploring numerous Dilmun sites over a period of fifteen years. Bibby was also granted permission to conduct a brief excavation on Tarut Island on the Saudi Arabian coast, near the town of Qatif. Archeologists have identified evidence of human settlement on Tarut dating from approximately 7,000 years ago, making Tarut Island the oldest continuously-inhabited place on the planet.

Just as Geoffrey Bibby was looking for Dilmun, on one occasion, I was looking for something, too: the Seef Mall.

Bahrain boasts a number of colossal, multi-story shopping malls where customers can buy virtually anything under the sun. Gulf Arabs are some of the world's most avid consumers, consequently all the American, Asian and European chains have shops in these malls, and there's no annoying sales tax or Value Added Tax tacked onto the merchandise.

Non-Muslims can also purchase alcoholic beverages and pork in Bahrain; sale and consumption of both are banned on the other side of the causeway. This situation was not so different from what I had known back in Kentucky. My town was "dry," meaning that sale and consumption of alcoholic beverages were not permitted. Towns on the other side of the Ohio River, however, were "wet." Kentuckians crossed the bridge to buy their booze.

The Seef Mall is Bahrain's second largest mall. It covers 100,000 square meters (almost a million square feet) and features two multiplex cinemas, an indoor ice-skating rink and family-oriented entertainment programs.

I was looking for the Seef Mall when I was working as a contractor for Saudi Aramco, the world's largest producer and exporter of crude oil. By this time, the causeway between Saudi Arabia and Bahrain had been opened to the public.

One weekend, I decided to drive over to Bahrain to do some shopping and take in a movie on one of the big screens in the multiplex at the Seef Mall. Since there are no public cinemas in Saudi Arabia, people watch films on satellite television channels and on DVDs. It wasn't a decision to be taken on the spur of the moment since, even though I had a Saudi residence permit, it was invalid in Bahrain. Additionally, the automobile insurance I had was limited to Saudi Arabia. This meant that halfway across the bridge drivers had to stop for (1) inspection by Saudi Customs agents (2) purchase of the Bahraini visa and (3) enrollment in Bahraini auto insurance.

I knew that the Seef Mall was west of Manama, so I hadn't bothered to take a map of Bahrain. I expected that the route to such a highly-frequented place would be marked on the main highway crossing the island. I drove straight east, looking for the exit that would take me north to the mall. I kept driving. No sign. Finally, the skyscrapers in downtown Manama hove into sight. One of them, the 50-story Bahrain World Trade Center, inaugurated in 2008, is the first skyscraper in the world to integrate wind turbines into its design; they are expected to provide between 11% and 15% of the two towers' power consumption.

I knew I had gone too far, so I turned off the highway at the next exit and drove west on a narrow, paved road, still looking for the Seef Mall. Before long, I arrived at a dusty, decrepit village surrounded by date palm plantations; the inhabitants

25

eyed suspiciously my little Toyota Tercel with its KSA license plates and the name of my company stenciled on the doors. This was not the Seef Mall.

In frustration and annoyance, I turned around and drove all the way back to Saudi Arabia. The next morning, at the office, I recounted to my colleagues how I had been looking for the Seef Mall but couldn't find it. The men were compassionate, but several of the Saudi ladies found my misadventure highly amusing.

In my mind, however, it wasn't just embarrassment. This was a lesson learned. There are some places that are so well known that everybody assumes that everybody else knows where they are and how to get there. That was the case for the Seef Mall. Everybody in Bahrain and in nearby parts of Saudi Arabia had been to the Seef Mall so often that they could have driven to it in their sleep. And the management of the Bahraini highways had apparently not bothered to go to the expense of posting signs to the mall since they, too, assumed that anybody who wanted to go there had already been there.

Such was the conundrum; I was its victim.

"Are You Going to Saudi Arabia?"

The flight from Paris to Manama on Gulf Air was uneventful; thanks to a tailwind, we arrived ahead of time, a little after 7:00 PM. A hundred or so excited and voluble French backpackers occupied a large section of coach class. I chatted to a few of them in the departure lounge at Charles de Gaulle Airport before takeoff; they were on their way to a trek in Nepal. I've been a hiker for many years, and some of these tenderfeet seemed ill-prepared for the rigors awaiting them at 5,000 meters—16,000 feet—above sea level, but I refrained from dampening their enthusiasm.

Because I was traveling in business class, I enjoyed a delicious gourmet meal, preceded by champagne, accompanied by Meursault and followed by cognac—all excellent. The Sky Chef, whom I took to be British, had come around to take our orders, answer questions about the menu and bring us our meals. I complimented the crew on the high quality of the service as I deplaned.

Luggage of business class passengers was tagged for priority unloading, so I glided through customs in the Fast Track lane in just a couple of minutes.

The stamp in my passport not only showed the date of my arrival, but the legend, "Welcome to Business-Friendly Bahrain." That was the first time I had seen an advertising slogan on a passport stamp.

I had been told that somebody would be on hand at the airport to pick me up, but did not know who it might be. As I left customs, I was confronted with a swarm of drivers, each holding up a card with the name of an expected passenger. One of them, whom I took for an Indian, was holding up a sign that said "Mr. Ron." Since I didn't see my name on any other sign, and since I knew it was common in this part of the world to address people by their given names, I figured he must have been assigned to me, so I allowed him to load my suitcases onto the cart and lead the way out to his vehicle in the parking lot. After he loaded my luggage in the trunk and slammed it closed, we got into the car and backed out of the parking space. The driver then asked me where I was going. I hadn't the slightest idea—I figured that he should have known where he was supposed to be taking me—so we got out of the car and I opened my carry-on to check the paperwork for the name and address of the building where I was going to be living. At that point, Ashraf—I had learned that to be his name—asked me, "Are you going to Saudi Arabia?" "Not this time," I replied, "I'm staying in Bahrain." It then dawned on both of us simultaneously: he wasn't my driver and I wasn't his Ron. I abandoned Ashraf, grabbed the luggage cart and hot-footed it back into the terminal to try to find the person who was supposed to meet me. I looked over my shoulder and saw Ashraf attempting to find another parking space; somebody else had already snatched his.

As it turned out, the project manager himself had been waiting at the airport to meet me all along, but we had missed each other. He had, in fact, spotted someone he thought was me coming out of customs, but after he saw me leaving the terminal with Ashraf, he had assumed that one more Ron was yet to disembark. After a while, I saw that Ashraf had returned to his position to await his Ron anew.

I was assigned quarters in a recently-completed apartment building in a neighborhood called Juffair, a short drive from the training facility located near the airport. As is the custom in the Gulf countries, the apartment was colossal: the living room at least 50 square meters—over 500 square feet—in area, and a separate bedroom was almost as large as the living room. There was an entry hall, a fully-equipped kitchen, a bathroom with tub and toilet and a separate lavatory that was probably reserved for guests.

The living room had shiny floors; tiles of either polished marble or some kind of marble composite. Unfortunately, it would have been suicide to walk on the floor with wet feet; the surface was as slippery as ice. Fortunately, I had packed a pair of non-skid bedroom slippers. There was a gigantic flat-screen television and a DVD player, but almost no television channels of interest aside from the European version of CNN International and BBC World. I was surprised that I couldn't receive Al Jazeera English (AJE), based in nearby Qatar, which shows excellent documentaries and tends to cover stories the mainstream American media ignore, but then I realized that AJE's exercise of freedom of the press included criticism of the Bahrainis, so I thought that might explain its absence from the menu. I later learned that AJE was not "banned in Bahrain," but simply not included in the building's cable subscription.

In addition to a full-size refrigerator, a dish washer, a clothes washer and drier, a microwave and an oven, the kitchen was equipped with a toaster, an electric kettle, a coffee maker, a blender, an electric citrus press and something called an electric sandwich maker. The only problem was that there were only two electric outlets in the entire kitchen, both located close together on the wall behind a chessboard-sized counter space next to the elements of the stove. I plugged in the kettle and toaster for my morning tea and toast; there was no room left for anything else. So, if I wanted to experiment with the intriguing electric sandwich maker, I would have had to disconnect either the kettle or the toaster and store it elsewhere.

Furthermore, the refrigerator was located next to the kitchen door so, every time I wanted to open the refrigerator door, I had to close the kitchen door. It became quite clear to me that whoever designed the kitchen had either flunked out of architectural school or had never set foot in an actual kitchen.

The top two floors of the building were occupied by swimming pools—two of them, outdoor and indoor—a barbecue area, a couple of Jacuzzis and a conference center with a bank of computers. Staff, mostly from the Philippines and India, were on hand twenty-four hours a day, and the apartments were cleaned twice a week by a team of taciturn Ethiopian housemaids.

Unfortunately, the building was located a hundred feet or so from Bahrain's busiest thoroughfare, a six-lane expressway starting at the country's main commercial port and continuing straight across the island to the causeway and on to destinations in Saudi Arabia. Zoning? What zoning? I had an unobstructed view of the highway from both my bedroom and my living room. High-speed traffic whizzed by twenty-four hours a day; heavy-duty big rigs seemed to start their delivery runs from the port at 4:30 or five o'clock in the morning. Despite the thermal-pane glass in the windows and heavy curtains, the rumbling was present both day and night. The day after I moved in, I implored the manager to move me to an apartment on the "quiet" side of the building, but to no avail; there wouldn't any vacancies until mid-2011. And by then I would be long gone.

The Kingdom of Bahrain can be described as a constitutional monarchy with an active monarch.[4] Its bicameral National Assembly betrays a distinct influence of the United Kingdom in that the members of one chamber are appointed and those of the other chamber elected. Like the British House of Lords, the 40 members of the upper chamber, known as the Shura Council, are appointed by the king; like the House of Commons, the 40 members of the Council of Representatives are elected by absolute majority in single-member constituencies. Members of both houses serve four-year terms.

---

[4] In addition to Bahrain, constitutional monarchies with an active monarch include Bhutan, Jordan, Kuwait, Liechtenstein, Monaco, Morocco, Tonga and the United Arab Emirates.

One difference, however, is that Bahrain boasts a written constitution, whereas the British constitution is unwritten.

The legislative and municipal elections that were held the day before my arrival had transpired without any untoward incidents.

The elections were open and transparent and both men and women were eligible to vote and run for elective office.

As reported both by GlobalSecurity.org [5] and by General Sir Graeme Lamb, [6] in 1924 Bahrain witnessed its first municipal elections, which specifically permitted the participation of women. This progressive move placed Bahrain ahead of many other countries that had not yet enfranchised women. The right of Bahraini women to vote and run for elected office was confirmed in 1973.

For comparison, women did not gain the right to vote in France until 1944 and could not vote in federal elections in Switzerland until February 7, 1971.

General Lamb also notes that when Bahrain was elected head of the 61st session of the United Nations General Assembly in 2006, it appointed as president Sheikha Haya Rashed Al Khalifa, the first Middle Eastern woman to fill the role and only the

---

[5] GlobalSecurity.org. Bahrain: History
[6] "Don't lump Bahrain in with Libya and Syria," *The Times* [London], August 15, 2011.

third woman president in the history of the General Assembly.

To encourage citizens to vote, the government had installed polling booths in highly-frequented places such as shopping malls and even in the airport concourse. All Bahraini citizens carry national ID cards with an embedded microprocessor chip; voter fraud was virtually impossible, since nobody could vote more than once.

During the next few days after my arrival, I would see ubiquitous posters, billboards and bumper stickers left over from the campaign, still promoting the candidacy of the various contenders.

Although I did not see any women's faces on the campaign posters, six women did run for the forty seats in the Council of Representatives. One won; Latifa Al Qaoud, who had been elected in 2006, was reëlected.

Unlike in America, in the Bahraini elections there were no hanging chads, and ballot counting was not halted *in medias res* by a partisan Supreme Court; on the other hand, as in America, accusations were made by the opposition that some electoral districts had been gerrymandered to facilitate the victory of pro-government candidates.

The poor showing of female candidates in the polls led some to recommend implementation of a quota system to guarantee a designated number of seats for women in the legislature and local councils. This sounds more like Scandinavia than the Middle East!

In the results of the elections, after the runoff held on October 30, 2010, the Islamic National Accord Association, known as Al Wefaq, won 18 out of 40 seats and became the largest block in the Council of Representatives. In order to understand Bahrain and what is happening there today, it is important to keep in mind that Al Wefaq is the principal political organization representing the Shia Muslim population.

Shortly after the elections for the Council of Representatives, King Hamad appointed the 40 members of the Shura Council to serve until 2014. A total of 19 Shias were designated, including the speaker, Ali bin Salih al Salih. Four women were among the appointees, among them Nancy Khadouri, who is Jewish, and Hala Qarrisah, a Christian.

As for the House of Khalifa, its legitimacy in Bahrain has been established through a long and documented history extending back to 1783, when Ahmad Al Fateh bin Muhammad Al Khalifa became the first monarch.

Most of the other Gulf monarchies have long histories, too. Although the modern Kingdom of Saudi Arabia was formally created in 1932, control of the Arabian Peninsula by the House of Saud dates back to 1744, when Mohammed bin Abd Al Wahhab and Mohammed bin Saud formed a political and religious alliance, thereby establishing sovereignty of the Al Sauds.

The Al Thani family has been governing Qatar since the state's foundation in 1825; in the United Arab

Emirates, the ruling families date back as far as the mid-19th century in Sharjah, the late 18th century in Abu Dhabi and the early 20th century in Dubai.

Furthermore, the first country in the world to recognize the independence of the United States of America was the Kingdom of Morocco, on December 20, 1777, under the reign of King Mohammed III. The two countries signed a Treaty of Peace and Friendship in 1787. On July 18, 1987, each country issued postage stamps commemorating the 200th anniversary of the treaty.

Since the Lebanese Civil War deposed Beirut as the financial center of the Middle East, "Business-Friendly Bahrain" has been attempting to capture the title. But there's lots of evidence that Bahrain, too, has suffered the consequences of the global economic bust.

On one of my days off, one Friday morning, two colleagues and I drove to the extreme northwestern tip of the island to a fishing village called Budaiya.

We were traveling on Friday because the Bahraini weekend is Friday and Saturday. As mentioned previously, in Saudi Arabia the weekend is Thursday and Friday. And, for most of my life, the weekend has been Saturday and Sunday. Consequently, my body clock functioned in a constant state of dislocation. the time was always out of joint. Every morning, when I woke up, I would ask myself, is this a work day or a day off? Go back to sleep or get up? Dress up or dress down?

When we reached Budaiya we first stopped to gawk at a miniature Versailles left eerily vacant because of a dispute among the heirs of the deceased owner. Not far away on the horizon extended a development of at least half a dozen colossal structures around thirty stories each, most likely funded by wealthy Emirati or Saudi promoters inspired by the Dubai building boom and intended to be sold as condominium apartments. All the buildings were now abandoned half-finished, their steel skeletons revealing their nakedness, and the booms and jibs of their idle cranes jutting crazily askew. The Bahraini building boom had gone bust, too.

When I lived in Saudi Arabia I had learned that Bahrain was a place where non-Muslims could purchase both alcoholic beverages and pork products.

I soon discovered the "For Non-Muslims" room at the Al Jazira shopping mall, not far from where I lived. I bought bacon imported from Kenya and Danish ham and saw lots of British-type breakfast sausages. I also saw venison advertised for sale; when I asked for it one of the butchers disappeared into the meat locker and returned with an entire haunch of venison frozen solid; he offered to saw off as many slices as I wanted.

Of course, I couldn't neglect the local specialties, so I picked up some camel burgers as well. The meat is quite distinctive and the taste is unique, not at all like other meats, and it doesn't "taste like chicken." I quickly developed a liking for camel meat.

You can also buy filets of a particularly tasty fish caught in the Gulf and known locally as *hamour*; in English, its name is the brown-spotted grouper, but *hamour* sounds more appetizing to me. Shakespeare rightly asked, "What's in a name?" I went on the internet and found some recipes for cooking *hamour*.

The recipes were posted by Aramcons, the American petroleum technicians and engineers and their families who arrived in Saudi Arabia in the late 1930's. In order to attract the Americans, King Abdulaziz granted them certain privileges, including the right for women to drive inside the walled cantonment nicknamed "the Camp" at Dhahran and authorization to import pork. The Aramcons were also permitted to distill alcohol from sugar and yeast for their personal use and were provided with an instructional pamphlet known as *The Blue Flame*, explaining the procedure. The homebrewed product was nicknamed *sidiki*, Arabic for "little friend." Both the *sidiki* and the pork privileges were subsequently revoked, and *The Blue Flame* became a collector's item.

Islam is slightly ambivalent about the consumption of alcohol.[7] Two texts from the Quran bear this out. One verse states that alcoholic drinks possess "a great sin and some benefit for men, but the sin is

---

[7] The word "alcohol" is derived from the Arabic word, *al-ghawl*, meaning "spirit," and the French word for "still" is *alembic*, from the Arabic word, *āl-anbyq*.

greater than their benefit." Another passage admonishes Muslims not to pray to God if they are drunk. My own non-Islamic view is that Islam unequivocally recognizes some good in alcoholic beverages, such as the benefits to the heart of moderate consumption of red wine, but severely condemns drunkenness. However, since some people are unable to draw the line between healthiness and drunkenness, and some others—alcoholics—consume alcohol in a compulsive and uncontrolled manner, most Islamic countries simply prohibit the consumption of alcoholic beverages altogether.

Many of the American families remained in Saudi Arabia; today, third-generation Aramcons are working in Dhahran and elsewhere in the Kingdom.

Schadenfreude

It was seven o'clock in the morning. I was watching a rerun of a Charlie Rose interview on the television when I heard some louder than usual rumbling outside. I drew the curtains and was surprised to see slate black clouds against a grey welkin. Then I saw a lightning bolt. I heard thunder. It was raining in Bahrain. It was raining really hard, a real cloudburst. I could hear small hailstones peppering the window, too. And then the television reception conked out. Goodbye, Charlie!

According to meteorological data, it only rains in Bahrain from November through March. Rainfall averages 18 millimeters each month during this period. The rest of the year, the sun shines all the time and there's no rain at all.

The previous day one of my colleagues, his wife and I had visited the Bahraini National Museum, a two-story, ultra-modern, functional building housing exhibits cover 6,000 years ranging from prehistory to the 21st century. The most interesting exhibits to me were in the rooms devoted to the Dilmun civilization and culture and the exhibits depicting the lifestyle of Bahrain's pre-industrial past.

Two rooms are devoted to Dilmun. One of them features an actual burial mound around 4,000 years old. Part of the mound has been cut away like a slice of cake revealing the layers and structure of its interior. The tomb itself held a skeleton, and terra cotta jars of foods for the hereafter had been stacked nearby. Around the tomb a low stone wall was built;

another stone wall had been constructed further out. The structure had then been then covered with soil.

Bahrain has the world's largest concentration of these tumuli—as many as 75,000 of them. They extend as far as the eye can see in the western part of the island along the highway that leads to the causeway. An additional 2,500 Dilmun burial mounds have been identified in and around Dhahran on the mainland of the Arabian Peninsula approximately 50 kilometers (30 miles) from Bahrain.

The similarities of these Dilmun tumuli to the Neolithic dolmens in France and elsewhere in Europe were obvious to me; the periods of their construction were contemporaneous. Both structures functioned as burial chambers. The only differences are that, whereas the Dilmun people normally buried one body in each mound, the Europeans buried as many as 150 or more bodies inside the tombs and used much larger stones to construct them. If the dolmen-makers had covered their burial chamber, which seems likely, the rain and winds have had several millennia to wash the soil away.

Maps in the museum show how the Dilmun people conducted an active maritime commerce extending throughout the Gulf and the Arabian Sea to the Indian subcontinent. An overland trade route reached as far as the Levant and pre-Hellenic Greece.

We saw a number of showcases displaying the famous Dilmun seals. The museum gift shop sells framed reproductions of some of the seals, including the Beer Drinkers seal that served as the model for my gold pendant, but they do not sell the pendants themselves. I was told that *Looking for Dilmun* was out of print and not for sale either. I later went online and ordered a second-hand paperback copy from Amazon in the United Kingdom. The price: one penny. On the cover: a photograph of the Beer Drinkers, just like the one I was wearing around my neck. The image is ubiquitous.

People in the Dilmun civilization had also mastered the art of smelting copper, using the metal to forge tools, implements and weapons.

Most of the upper floor of the museum is devoted to a series of life-like, three-dimensional reconstructions depicting traditional Bahraini activities. You can see the mattress maker, the baker, the carpenter, the tobacconist and the locksmith plying their trades in their shops. A larger tableau recreates the life of the Bahraini pearl fishermen, who set out for three-to four-month long voyages to dive for pearls in the Gulf. Other displays recreate daily life in a traditional Bahraini household, marriage customs, schools and folk medicine. All these exhibits are extremely well-designed and labeled in both English and Arabic.

When I was in Saudi Arabia, on the rare days it rained, the streets and low-lying highways always flooded because the government had not installed any storm sewers; since it rained so seldom, the authorities probably determined that it was a waste of money—it wasn't economically justifiable.

I looked out the window again; it appeared that the Bahrainis hadn't installed storm sewers either, since there was a gigantic traffic jam in three of the six lanes of the superhighway. Scores of the heavy-duty trucks that awakened me in the middle of the night, as well as hundreds of automobiles, had ground to a complete halt or were crawling forward at a snail's pace, stranded in the flood. Imagining the drivers' discomfiture, I burst out laughing.

The Germans have a word for it: *schadenfreude.*

Sunnis, Shias, Christians and Jews

The world's billion and a half Muslims are divided into two main denominations, Sunnis and Shias. Like Protestants and Catholics, Sunni and Shia Muslims share most of the same beliefs and religious practices but, like Protestants and Catholics, each has its own specificities. Shia Muslims, for example, attribute a particularly important role to the Prophet Mohammed's cousin and son-in-law, Ali.

Over 80% of the world's Muslims are Sunni. Most of the rest are Shia, although there are, as in Christianity, smaller sects. Among them are the Alawites, the Ismaili, the Ahmadiyya and the Sufi. In Saudi Arabia, as in most Muslim countries, Sunnis are the overwhelming majority, around 90% of the population. The Shia minority is concentrated in the oil-rich Eastern Province, mostly in and around the coastal towns of Qatif, Safwa and Awamiyah, in the area around Hofuf and on Tarut Island.

In Bahrain, however, as in Iran and Iraq, Shias are a majority. Although it is generally assumed and reported in the media that Shias make up 65 to 75 percent of the population, research conducted in 2009 by political scientist Justin Gengler indicates otherwise. On April 5, 2011, Gengler published his findings in his blog, Religion and Politics in Bahrain: Facts on the Ground. His research revealed that:

> Bahraini Shi'is comprised 58% of my survey sample, Sunnis 42%--a ratio far different from that commonly cited.

Gengler also published an ethnic map of Bahrain showing the geographical segregation of Bahrain's two communities. Muharraq Island and Al Rifa, for example, are predominantly Sunni; the Sitra Peninsula and Budaiya are overwhelmingly Shia and villages such as Hamad Town and Isa Town are ethnically mixed. Gengler concludes:

> In sum, there is every reason to believe that the Shi'a of Bahrain today comprise less than 60% of the country's total population. Not only does this estimate represent a vast improvement over current educated guesses reported in media and elsewhere, but it calls attention to the pace and scope of Bahrain's program of politically-motivated naturalization of Sunnis. [8]

Unlike Iran and Iraq, Bahrain is a kingdom, and King Hamad and most, but not all, cabinet ministers are Sunnis. Following the parliamentary elections, the Shia opposition had emerged as the largest bloc in the island Council of Representatives.

One of the things that I like to do is figure out who is Sunni is and who is Shia. The game is akin to trying to figure out who is a Catholic and who is a Protestant from external appearances alone.[9] But there are telltale signs. Many Shia men wear a silver ring inlaid with a semi-precious stone—agate, turquoise, opal or carnelian. This is because of a

---

[8] "Facts on the Ground: A Reliable Estimate of Bahrain's Sunni-Shi'i Balance, and Evidence of Demographic Engineering." http://bahrainipolitics.blogspot.com

[9] In France, many Protestants wear the Huguenot Cross, an eight-pointed Maltese Cross with *fleurs-de-lis* between each arm. At the bottom is a pendant dove, its beak pointed downward.

tradition that Ali wore such rings on his hands. These rings are always silver because, in Islam, only women wear gold jewelry. Wealthy Bahraini and Saudi men may display their affluence discretely by wearing platinum wristwatches.

The gemstones are quarried and polished at Shia religious sites in Iran and Iraq. Some Shias attribute special medicinal or curative powers and "vibrational properties" to these stones; Sunnis dismiss this practice as unscientific and akin to sorcery.

For conservative Sunnis, the Shias are not part of mainstream Islam at all, but an offshoot based on blood-letting, idolatry and martyrdom, all of which are anathema to them. In the eyes of many Sunnis, Ali and his son Hussein assume an importance equal to the Prophet Mohammed himself.

Despite their differences, in most parts of the Muslim world, Shia and Sunni Muslims have co-existed peacefully, just as Catholics and Protestants in Christian countries. From time to time, however, sectarian rivalry leads to conflict and bloodshed. Catholics and Protestants fought each other during the Wars of Religion in 16th century France and the Troubles in Northern Ireland in the 20th century. Likewise, bloody conflict between Sunni and Shia broke out in Iraq after the fall of the Saddam Hussein regime.

Since Ali plays such an important role in Shia Islam, it is not surprising that "Ali" seemed to be the most common man's name among Shias; around a quarter of the trainees were so named.

Like the Saudis, Bahrainis, both Shia and Sunni, have multiple names; the first is the given name and is followed by the first names of the father and grandfather and the family name. The word *bin* after the first name indicates "son of" and *bint* means "daughter of." Some large families or clans are referred to as tribes: the Al Saud tribe is the ruling family in Saudi Arabia as is the Al Khalifa tribe in Bahrain. Gulf Arabs carry their genealogy with them at all times in their names.

With respect to the women, the Shia Bahrainis seemed to dress less conservatively than their Sunni sisters. I noticed that lot of Bahraini women wear what we might call western dress, so I supposed that they must be Shia.

And the veil. What about the veil? The word "veil" is not mentioned anywhere in the Quran, and nowhere is it indicated that women must cover their face.[10] The wearing of the veil is simply a custom practiced in certain Muslim countries, but not in others. The veil has nothing to do with Islam; in fact, the veiling of women was not an Islamic innovation at all, but a Persian and Byzantine-Christian custom that some Muslims adopted.

---

[10] "Does the Quran Require Women to Wear the Veil?"
http://middleeast.about.com/od/religionsectarianism/f/me080209.htm

What the Quran does state is that both women and men should both dress modestly. That's it!

The problem with the veil is not that Islam requires it, but that many Muslim women in some countries have been brainwashed or browbeaten into thinking that they must wear a veil. Most but not all of the Saudi women and almost all the Bahraini women with whom I worked did not wear veils but dressed just like women in Paris or Washington or wore an *abaya*—the word means "cloak" in Arabic—an ample, loose overgarment, essentially a robe-like dress. Most of these ladies did not cover their faces.

Insofar as wearing a veil is concerned, in theory, a Muslim woman has the right to choose what she wishes, just as she can choose to wear a skirt or slacks.

A veil is not a scarf, although there seems to some confusion between the two. Indonesia is the most populous Muslim country in the world. Eighty-eight percent of its population of over 200 million people are Muslim. Most Indonesian Muslim women wear a headscarf, but not a veil.

When I was on a photographic assignment in January 1980 documenting traditional architecture in Asir Province in the southwest corner of Saudi Arabia close to Yemen, I saw women at the wheel of pickup trucks wearing brightly colored dresses embellished with elaborate embroidery. No veils. No *abayas*. Driving. Saudi Arabia.

If Bahraini women rarely wear a veil, many veiled women can be seen in the shopping malls, especially during the weekends, when hordes of Saudis migrate across the causeway. The Saudi women will be shopping while the menfolk furtively ogle scantily-clad expatriate women who appear to have no concern for the sensitivities or taboos of their hosts. Also, although many Bahraini women wear the long, black *abaya*, it seems to me that the ones that Shia ladies wear are decorated with colorful, decorative embroidery, whereas the Sunnis seem to prefer a more puritanical plain black.

Furthermore, among the nomadic Tuaregs of North Africa, who are Muslim, the custom is for men to cover their faces with a veil, not the women.

The conclusion is that dress codes for Muslims are a lot more complex than most non-Muslims think and defy oversimplification and stereotyping.

Unlike Saudi Arabia, Bahrain observes religious tolerance and members of all religions may practice their faiths freely and openly.

Approximately 9% of the Bahraini population is Christian; among them are an estimated 1,000 Christians who hold Bahraini nationality. As previously mentioned, a Bahraini Christian woman serves in the Shura Council. The Arab Christians are mostly the decedents of recent immigrants from Palestine, Jordan and Iraq, where Christian communities have existed since the beginning of the first and second centuries. Europeans, Americans,

Filipinos and Indians make up the remainder of the expatriate Christian community.

Although there are numerous Christian churches in Bahrain, there are none in Saudi Arabia, even though there was a significant Christian presence in the Arabian Peninsula before the arrival of Islam. The ruins of a 4th century Nestorian Christian church were unearthed in 1986 near the town of Jubail, on the Gulf coast about 100 kilometers (60 miles) northwest of Dammam.

Bahrain currently is host to a Jewish community of some forty members, descendents of Jews who originated from Iraq. A small synagogue is located on Sasa'ah Avenue in Manama, but it is currently unused because a *minyan* of ten Jewish adults required for prayer can only rarely be mustered. Nevertheless, Bahrain is one of the only Gulf countries to host a Jewish community or synagogue. The Bahraini Jewish community also maintains a small Jewish cemetery.

In 2008, a Bahraini Jewish woman, Houda Ezra Nonoo, was appointed by King Hamad to be Bahrain's ambassador to the United States and Canada.[11]

Whatever their differences in detail and ritual, the three great monotheistic religions are all united in worshiping the same divinity, and the three coexist

---

[11] In 2013, Ambassador Nonoo was replaced by Bahrain's defense attaché in Washington, Lt. Col. Abdullah bin Muhammed Al Khalifa. A Bahraini Christian woman, Alice Thomas Yusuf Samaan, was appointed ambassador to the Court of St. James's in London in 2011 and to the Netherlands in 2014.

peacefully in Bahrain. During the protests that began in February 2011, Sunnis were not attacked because they were Sunni and vice versa; the demonstrations were political and economic in nature, not religious. There were Shia and Sunni trainees in my classes, and I never detected any signs of disaccord among them.

It may appear surprising that in all the time I spent in Saudi Arabia and Bahrain, not one person attempted to convert me to Islam, either by the word or by the sword! On a few occasions people offered me brochures explaining the principles of Islam, but most of the people I worked with knew that I already understood the fundamental tenants of Islam and that I respected their faith.

Sometimes I was able to use my knowledge of Islam in a teaching situation. I knew, for example, that Muslims abhor suicide and believe that such an act condemns one's soul to hell. I also knew that Saudi Arabia has one of the world's worst records for highway deaths, 29.0 fatalities per 100,000 inhabitants per year. On more than one occasion, I admonished my trainees to drive carefully, because reckless driving could be considered suicidal behavior. I hoped my sermonizing produced the desired effect.

By contrast, Bahraini drivers, both men and women, are required to attend classes and pass a rigorous test in order to obtain their driver's license, so their record for traffic deaths and accidents is much better, 12.1 fatalities per 100,000 inhabitants per year, approximately the same as the rate in the United States.[12]

On other occasions, I used my knowledge of Islam to encourage smokers to quit the habit.

According to Saudi government statistics, the country is the world's fourth largest importer of tobacco; six million Saudis spend about 30 million Saudi riyals (about $8 million) per day on cigarettes.

During the holy month of Ramadan, Muslims are expected to forgo food, drink, sexual intercourse—and smoking—during the daylight hours. I reminded smokers that, since they had demonstrated the ability to give up smoking during Ramadan, they might as well continue after Eid al Fitr, the celebration marking the end of Ramadan.

There's actually more to this than appears at first glance. Not only is alcohol proscribed in Islam, but are all addictive substances, including—at least theoretically—nicotine. The concept behind this is that an addiction is a form of slavery or servitude. For Muslims, humans are only expected to be servitors of God; the name "Abdullah" means, literally, "servant of God."

Following this precept, in the years from 1928 to 1930, Saudi religious police, the *mutaween*, waged a

---

[12] *Global Status Report on Road Safety*, Geneva, Switzerland, World Health Organization, 2009.

vigorous anti-smoking campaign. King Abdulaziz (known as Ibn Saud) agreed at the time to prohibit tobacco imports, but did not formally implement the ban. I was told, however, that even in the 1990's, cigarettes were not sold openly in the ultra-conservative stronghold of Buraida.

Bahrain implemented draconian restrictions on smoking in public in April 2009. The government outlawed advertising of cigarettes and even imposed a fine on smoking in private vehicles if children were present

In a return to the anti-smoking attitude of the late 1920s, Saudi authorities banned smoking in all government offices and most public places, including restaurants, coffee shops, supermarkets and shopping malls on July 30, 2012, according to press reports. The government also prohibited the sale tobacco products to anyone under the age of 18.

Shopping

The first day on the job I learned that the trainers were expected to wear neckties. Since I hadn't worn them when working on the other side of the causeway, I hadn't packed any of my pricy Hermès ties. A colleague came to my rescue and lent me one of his. Another colleague told me that I could buy ties upstairs at the Mega Mart.

The Mega Mart is about ten minutes on foot from my residence, on Al Shabab Avenue, known to all expatriates as "the Strip" because of the plethora of gaudy signs identifying the fast-food joints crowded next to each other on both sides of the street.

The groceries and foodstuffs in the Mega Mart are on the ground floor, and a rubber-surfaced moving ramp whisks shoppers effortlessly to the upper story, where they can find everything from stereos to pots and pans—and neckties. You might call the Mega Mart the Mini Costco.

The necktie selection wasn't very extensive, but I picked out three that I thought were suitable for work and that matched my blazer and sport coat. You can imagine my surprise when I checked the price tags to see what the ties were going to cost me: one of them was 3.500 Bahraini dinars.[13] That corresponded to $9.28 or €7.02. Another tie cost 2.900 BD ($7.69 or €5.81), and the third one cost me all of 900 fils ($2.38 or €1.80). Eat your heart out, Hermès!

---

[13] Abbreviated BD, the dinar is divided not into 100 units but into 1,000 units, called fils.

61

I have always liked to eat dates. When I was growing up in Kentucky, I remember the dates were imported from Iraq. Dates have been a staple food in the Gulf for millennia. In Saudi Arabia I discovered that dates also carry a quasi-religious significance; traditionally, they are the first food eaten to break the fast during the holy month of Ramadan. Arabic has several different words for "date" depending on their degree of ripeness. *Rutab* is the term for freshly-harvested dates; *tamur* refers to ripe, sun-dried dates, the type most familiar to Westerners.

The late Sir Wilfred Thesiger lived with the Bedouins and spent the five years between 1945 and 1950 journeying with them throughout the Empty Quarter—the Rub al Khali—the largest sand desert in the world, comprising most of the southern third of the Arabian Peninsula. In his account of his experiences, *Arabian Sands,* published in 1959, Thesiger observes that dates and camel's milk comprised the staple diet of the Bedouins. He and his companions often survived for days on just a handful of dates and a cup of camel's milk.

Not only are dates sweet and tasty but their nutritional value is exceptionally high. They are rich in carbohydrates and many other essential nutrients including potassium and magnesium, along with high levels of the B-vitamins thiamine, riboflavin, niacin, pantothenic acid and B6. Because the Bedouins believe that dates are helpful in relieving and preventing pain in the joints—perhaps due to the high level of potassium—they have dubbed them "nails for the knees."

The cultivated date palm is believed to have originated in the area around the Gulf. It is considered one of the first indications of the transformation of society from hunter-gatherers to sedentary farmers. Hundreds of date cultivars exist in Saudi Arabia, Bahrain and other parts of the Middle East and, today, several dozen varieties are cultivated commercially.

In the United States, dates are grown commercially in the Coachella Valley of California. The *medjool* variety was chosen after an agronomist was sent on a mission to North Africa early in the 20th century to collect samples. Experiments determined that the *medjool* was best suited to the soil and atmospheric conditions of the California desert.

Bateel, a chain of upscale boutiques specializing in dates and sweets, is headquartered in Saudi Arabia and has retail outlets throughout the Gulf, the Far East and in London. Bateel's online catalogue offers no fewer than 28 different varieties of dates; in Bahrain, you can buy all of them at the Bateel boutique in the posh Al A'Ali Mall.

My favorite date is the *barhi*, amber-colored, round and wrinkled; biting into one is like biting into a ball of honey.

The most expensive dates are known as *agwa* or *ajwa*; they're about the size and color of a truffle. Their high cost—over $20.00 per kilogram—is because they can only be grown in the *terroir* in and around the city of Medina in Saudi Arabia and because the Prophet Mohammed was particularly fond of them.

In earlier days, Bahrain was known as the island of a million date palms, so I expected to discover some new varieties. I finally found some Bahraini dates at the Carrefour supermarket, which is the anchor of the Bahrain City Centre mall. The French retail giant is the world's second largest after Wal-Mart and is heavily invested in the Gulf. The gargantuan Bahrain City Centre mall dwarfs the Al A'Ali Mall Mall next to it and, extending over 450,000 square meters (almost five million square feet), is over four times larger than the Seef Mall. For comparison, the Mall of America in Bloomington, MN, has an area of 390,000 square meters (4,200,000 square feet).

The best Bahraini dates I discovered were *safawi*. They're not round like the *barhi*, but rectangular and dark, almost black, and they are chewy. I also bought boxes of *mabroom* dates stuffed with almonds. These are made by splitting the date lengthwise, removing the pit and replacing it with a whole almond. The result is a treat that is both chewy and crunchy.

The best thing about shopping in Bahrain—or elsewhere in the Gulf—is that you can find food products from all over the world in the same store. Every grocery store and supermarket in Bahrain is like a Dean & DeLuca. Logs of Kraft Cracker Barrel cheddar lie on the shelves side-by-side with packages of Bridel French emmenthal, and boxes of Triscuit crackers from America cohabit peacefully on the same shelf between Walkers Scottish oat cakes and genuine Jewish matzo. Butter is imported from Wales, Ireland, England, New Zealand, Denmark and…Saudi Arabia: the Al Marai dairy in Saudi Arabia is the world's largest, and its 14,000 Holsteins graze indoors in air-conditioned comfort.

As with dates, honey has been a part of my daily diet since childhood. And after reading William Duffy's bestselling *Sugar Blues*, published in 1986, I swore off refined sugar and artificial sweeteners altogether and replaced them with honey.

Like dates, honey plays an important role in the Muslim diet because its healthful qualities are described in the Quran. Certain types of wild honey are harvested in Yemen and in Asir Province of Saudi Arabia and sold in specialized shops in the Gulf countries at prices sometimes approaching $100 a kilogram. The price is justified because many people believe that this wild honey lowers high blood pressure.

I was pleased to find some unusual honeys at the Mega Mart. The first exotic honey I found was imported from India. The label assured the purchaser that the honey was collected from "the best-known forest sources of the Himalayas and the Sundarbans." (The Sundarbans, I learned, are tidal mangrove forests located along the Bay of Bengal.) It seemed to me that the taste had a hint of turmeric.

I also bought honey from South Australia; according to the label, it was made from "delicate eucalyptus blossoms and ground flora." But as impressive as the subtle flavor of eucalyptus in the Australian honey was its plastic squeeze bottle. The Aussies had figured out a way to incorporate a plastic valve into the pouring spout that successfully cut off the flow of honey as soon as you stopped squeezing the bottle, making it completely spillproof.

During the long Eid al Adha holiday, celebrated at the end of the month of the Hajj pilgrimage to Mecca, I caught a cold, probably a consequence of the heavy-duty, industrial-strength air conditioning in my apartment, so I went down to the pharmacy on the Strip to get some cold medicine. The cough syrup the Bahraini pharmacist recommended was something from Germany called Prospan®. She assured me that she had received "very good feedback" about this product, so I bought a bottle. What I discovered about Prospan® when I got home is not only that it is alcohol-free (thus making it Muslim-friendly) and free of sugar and artificial sweeteners (making it Ronald-friendly), but that it is an entirely natural product whose active ingredient is the dry extract of a European medicinal ivy whose scientific name is *Hedra Helix* L. Of course, I had to find out more about this miraculous herb, so I promptly went onto the internet. I learned that the common name for this plant is English Ivy. The French call it *lierre grimpant* or *l'Herbe de St. Jean*. There's no doubt that I have seen this plant during my many hikes in the area around Paris—it will frequently cover an entire wall of a farmhouse. I thought that during one of my next walks I could harvest some of the leaves to concoct my own cough suppressant.

Bahrain, like its next-door neighbor Saudi Arabia, is a "dry," country, which means that the sale of alcoholic beverages to Muslims is prohibited. But unlike Saudi Arabia, Bahrain has "bottle shops" the euphemism for stores located discretely in out-of-the-way places where non-Muslims can purchase beer, wine and spirits. I was surprised to discover that one of these stores was stocked with some real English ales. Since I am a member of Les Amis de la Bière, a French organization of beer connoisseurs, I lost no time in purchasing one bottle each of Adnams Southwold Bitter, Adnams Broadside and Young's Double Chocolate Stout. The irony of all this is that I wouldn't have been able to purchase those English ales in either France or America, since they aren't exported to those countries, but I was able to purchase them in "alcohol-free" Bahrain. Over the next few days I tasted each of the three and decided to order a case of the chocolate stout for home delivery but, alas, it was out of stock. He who hesitates is lost.

The bottle shops also have a good assortment of red and white wines from Europe, Australia, South Africa and America and the usual sprits—whiskies, gins and the like. Despite the absence of sales taxes or Value Added Taxes, most of the merchandise in these shops is not inexpensive; I saw a bottle of what looked like an unexceptional Minervois red for the equivalent of 12 euros. In France you could buy a similar bottle for half that.

It is unwise to drink and drive in Bahrain. According to the U.S. State Department, any sign of having consumed alcohol may be taken as prima facie evidence of driving under the influence and can result in a fine of up to 1,000 Bahraini dinars (about $2,700). You can also be arrested for using a cell phone while driving.

Not only do the bottle shops provide home delivery to their customers, but so do many other small businesses in Bahrain. I always took my shirts to the Dolphin Dry Cleaners to be washed, ironed and folded. It cost me 400 fils per shirt—a little over a dollar. And they delivered. The Mega Mart also delivered groceries straight to my apartment at no extra charge.

Bahrain is a petroleum-producing country, the first country in the Gulf to produce and export crude oil. Consequently, gasoline only costs 100 fils a liter. That converts to €0.10 a liter or about half a dollar a gallon, so it should not be surprising that so many Bahrainis—both male and female—can be observed at the wheel of gas-guzzling Mercedes-Benz, Jaguars and Bentleys. Behemoth SUV's such as Cadillac Escalades and Range Rovers seem to be particularly popular in Bahrain, and Ferraris and Lamborghinis are not rare sights on the streets of the island kingdom.

If you run out of cash in Bahrain, there's no problem: most stores accept credit cards from anywhere in the world. But you can do more with your card in Bahrain than shop. One day I noticed a high-tech ATM machine: you insert your credit card, punch in your PIN number, and the machine will not only disgorge Bahraini dinars, but euros and dollars as well.

About the only item I was surprised not to find in Bahrain is the famous handmade Aleppo soap, *Savon d'Alep* in French. This may well be the world's oldest soap, since it has been made in Aleppo, Syria, since time immemorial. An entirely natural product, it is made from only four ingredients: olive oil, water, lye and laurel oil. After the soap is hardened and cut into small bars, it is cured for a year in aging cellars before going on sale. I've been using this soap exclusively for several years and find that it helps prevent the skin from chapping and drying. One characteristic of Aleppo soap that enables consumers to distinguish the real from the fake is that, like the "99 44/100% pure" Ivory soap of yesteryear, real Aleppo soap floats. The Crusaders discovered this soap in the Middle Ages and brought the recipe back to France, where it became the inspiration for the well-known *Savon de Marseille*. I had no trouble finding Aleppo soap in Paris, and thought it would be easy to find in Bahrain. It wasn't.

Kenyon's Law

The approximate number of Dilmun burial mounds erected in Bahrain between 2,200 and 1,700 BC: 75,000. The approximate number that have been excavated professionally: 1,000. The approximate percentage that have been plundered: 99%.

The number of stores in the Bahrain City Centre mall: 330, spread out over three floors. The number that I shopped: five. I bought a new electric shaver at the Sharaf DG consumer electronics store; some toiletries at Boots the Chemist, a British chain; a pair of swim trunks at Wave Pro and a bottle of Annick Goutal fragrance at the Al Hawaj Parfumerie. And groceries at Carrefour.

The approximate number of fast-food joints on the Strip: thirty-five, by my count. Hungry Bahrainis and expatriates can choose among Chili's (home of the Big Mouth Burgers®); Burger King; Curry Country (a Bahraini-based chain specializing in Asian food); Hardee's; DQ (formerly known as Dairy Queen); Papa John's Pizza (nope, it's not Italian, but 100% American—John Schnatter started it in Jeffersonville, Indiana); Magic Wok (founded by Sutas Pipatjarasgit in Toledo, Ohio, in 1983); McDonalds; locally-owned Mashawi Al Abraaj; Nando's (a South-Africa based chain specializing in Portuguese and Mozambican cuisine); Zyng Asian Grill (a Montreal-based "Asian-inspired" chain); TCBY (once known as The Country's Best Yogurt); Bahrain-based Isfahani Persian Food; Costa Coffee (an upscale British-based competitor of Starbucks); Caribou Coffee (headquartered in Minneapolis, Minnesota); Fuddruckers ("World's Greatest

Hamburgers."); Atlanta-based Marble Slab Dairy ("The Freshest Ice Cream on Earth"); Cinnabon ("World-famous Cinnamon Rolls") and its associated coffee bar Seattle's Best Coffee; Freshberry Frozen Yogurt (based in Tulsa, Oklahoma); KFC (previously Colonel Harlan Sanders's Kentucky Fried Chicken); Popeye's (originally located in Arabi, Louisiana, across the Mississippi from New Orleans); Subway; coffee franchiser Second Cup ("Uniquely Canadian"); Steak Escape ("Home of America's favorite cheesesteak." But what's a "cheesesteak?"); BR ("Your Neighborhood Ice Cream Store," once known as Baskin-Robbins); SAJ Express (a Dubai-based chain specializing in Lebanese food); Le Bateau Café (which appears to be the only independent restaurant on the Strip); Starbucks; The Pizza Company (it's not based in Italy, either, but in Thailand); Sumo Sushi & Bento (also based in Dubai); Pizza Inn (from a very un-Italian sounding place called The Colony, Texas, but maybe the "colonists" were Italian); Moti Mahal (an upscale, London-based chain specializing in "innovative Indian tandoori cuisine"); Quiznos (with its toasted sandwiches); Hakisushi (this one, also, appears to be locally owned) and Romano's Macaroni Grill ("Fresh. Simple. Authentic." Dallas, Texas).

The number of these restaurants that I ate in: two. A colleague and his wife treated me to dinner at Romano's Macaroni Grill for my birthday; I enjoyed delicious grilled salmon and steamed vegetables. No macaroni. I often stopped at the Cinnabon for an expresso and a wickedly delicious Minibon®. I am afraid that if I consumed a full-sized Cinnabon® Classic, I'd collapse from a massive coronary and die on the spot, but a Minibon I can handle. Most meals I prepared at home.

The number of news channels I could access on the satellite television system before the cable guys came around to install the new converter: five—CNN, BBC World, Sky News from the U.K., Bloomberg and CNBC.

The number of news channels I could receive after they installed the new box: ten. I almost went ecstatic with joy, zapping happily between the previous five and Fox News, AJE, Euronews and Orbit News, the last of which—unbelievably—carried a selection of American programs mostly from MSNBC, enabling me to watch some progressive news programs to balance the neo-conservative Fox News. Plus, there was a comedy channel that broadcast Jay Leno's Tonight Show every night along with the Colbert Report and Jon Stewart's Daily Show.

But this state of bliss only lasted three days.

The technicians came around while I was at work and removed the new box and remote control.

The number of news channels I now had: one. CNN was all that was left. This was additional confirmation of what I call "Kenyon's Law," which postulates: *Every time the technicians come around to "improve" the current status, the result is worse than before.*

I had always thought that the United States was the only country whose paper money was all of the same size—making life difficult for the blind and the visually impaired. I was wrong. Bahraini banknotes are all the same size, too. But the Bahrainis included sets of parallel raised lines at the top right hand corner of each banknote to enable the blind to distinguish the half-dinar note (one line), the one-dinar note (two lines), the five-dinar note (three lines), the ten-dinar note (four lines) and the twenty-dinar note (five lines).

Dilmun and Ashura

I wrote previously that I had read *Looking for Dilmun*, the late Geoffrey Bibby's 1969 study of the lost civilization of Dilmun that was centered on the island of Bahrain. Dilmun's power extended to adjacent parts of the Arabian Peninsula and its merchant adventurers traded as far afield as India, Mesopotamia and the Levant. Today I, too, was looking for Dilmun and, like Bibby, I found it.

A colleague, his wife and I planned our itinerary to visit two quite different Dilmun sites, the Barbar Temple and the ruined city of Saar. Both sites, along with the tens of thousands of Dilmun burial mounds, are located on the northwest part of Bahrain, not far from the access ramp to the causeway. I had highlighted the two places on the Official Map of Bahrain that I had procured previously, and my colleague had programmed the GPS in the automobile to guide us to the Dilmun locations we were seeking.

Our first stop was the Barbar Temple which, we discovered, was logically located on Barbar Avenue. Bibby and his team of Danish archeologists, who conducted the first and only excavation of the site back in 1954, discovered no fewer than three temples all built on the same site, whose focus was an abundantly-flowing spring, reached by a set of stone steps, which have survived intact. The temple dates from the third millennium BC and was apparently dedicated to Enki, a god of both fresh water and wisdom; today, alas, the spring has run dry. The remaining vestiges of the temple are impressive: massive limestone megaliths, quarried on the neighboring Jidda Island and shipped over water and land to the temple site itself where stonecutters used copper tools to shape and fit the blocks into place.

Bibby and his fellow archeologists discovered a rich trove of Dilmun objects on the site of the Barbar Temple, including a cast bull's head and a votive copper statuette of a naked, clean-shaven man in a posture of supplication. Bibby's team also found seven of the Dilmun signature seals in the pool. Many of those artifacts we had seen on display during our previous visit to the Bahrain National Museum.

I was surprised to see what was once such a large temple standing alone, and when I returned home I plunged back into Bibby's book, which fell open to a page near the end of Chapter 11, where he speculates about the Barbar Temple:

> It began to look as though the Barbar temple was in truth a ziggurat, drowned in sand...I began to suspect that the Barbar temple might well be part of a much vaster complex. It had always seemed implausible that the temple had stood alone, out in the open country...It might be that it was the temple-tower of another city, the only structure which still rose above the encroaching sands...We have never dared to dig beyond the confines of the temple. For were we to find another city it would be beyond our resources to excavate it...[14]

---

[14] Bibby, Geoffrey. *Looking for Dilmun*, London, Pelican Books, 1972, page 252.

The second Dilmun site we visited was the ruined Bronze Age city of Saar. As at the Barbar Temple, a uniformed caretaker monitored the site from his booth. In contrast to the Barbar Temple, standing alone, Saar was once a fair-sized town located on a hill overlooking a wide plain.

As we wandered through the streets of ancient Saar, it was easy to imagine the lively activity animating the houses and shops that had once lined the streets of the town four thousand years ago. It must have been much like the hustle and bustle in one of Bahrain's busy souks today: merchants hawking their goods, tradesmen plying their wares, artisans—basket weavers, potters, blacksmiths, jewelers, bakers, mattress makers, grocers, fishmongers and brewers—practicing their trades and handicrafts. The town's spacious temple was also quite easy to identify.

But ancient Saar reminded me most of the martyred French village of Oradour-sur-Glane, near Limoges, in central France, which I had visited in October, 2010. On June 10, 1944, four days after the Allied Invasion of Normandy, the 644 inhabitants of the village—men, women, children and infants—were brutally massacred by troops of the Waffen SS, and the village was torched and burned to the ground. Saar and Oradour were eerily similar: barren, ruined stone walls and silent, sullen and deserted streets. It seemed quite plausible that Saar, too, had been set afire and razed by an enemy invader.

Like Oradour-sur-Glane, Saar has a modern twin. As we drove through the labyrinthine streets of the town, we spotted black flags—many of them bordered in blood red—flying from virtually every house and shop. We realized that the following day, December 16, 2010, was Ashura, the tenth day of the Islamic month of Muharram, the holiest day in the calendar for Shia Muslims.

The flags commemorated the bloody martyrdom of Imam Al Hussein. Banners, all black, inscribed with texts in Arabic were strung across the streets, and posters with images evoking the martyred Hussein had been attached to telephone poles. We could also hear the religious messages broadcast from loudspeakers mounted on the minarets of local mosques.

Ashura is not a joyful celebration, but a day of mourning that commemorates the martyrdom of Hussein, the son of Ali and grandson of the prophet Mohammed. Imam Al Hussein, as he is known to Shias, along with a band of seventy-two relatives and companions, was killed at the Battle of Karbala, in present-day Iraq, at the hands of the soldiers of Umayyad king Yazid on the tenth day of the month of Muharram in the year 61 AH, corresponding to October 2, 680 AD. It is said that Hussein was decapitated and his body mutilated.

It would be the same for the several other Shia villages we passed through: tens, scores, hundreds of black flags, dozens of black banners and innumerable posters. I spotted one banner in English, stretching fifty feet or so across the entire front of a large building in one village. Its inscription: *Imam Al Hussein's Revolution, Lessons and Examples.* Now there are quite a number of ways to interpret that message, and given Bahrain's recent history, not all of those interpretations are theological.

On Ashura itself, Shia men and boys march in a procession through the streets accompanied by drums, pounding their chests with their hands in a gesture of pain and sorrow, recreating the suffering endured by Imam Hussein and his companions.

Some Shia men practice a particular form of self-mutilation during Ashura. One of my friends' compatriots, a professional photographer, had been permitted to take pictures of these practices and had showed me some of the photographs she had taken, so I had an inkling of what Ashura was all about.

The photographer recounted how the men in the procession carried sharply-honed swords in their hands. (The women and children, excluded from the events, watched from the upper stories and the flat rooftops.) From time to time the procession stopped and the men would nick their scalps with their swords, allowing the blood to flow copiously over their faces and soaking their clothing. I saw pictures in which a celebrant's entire face was stained red with blood. Other celebrants performed a ritual flagellation, slashing their backs and shoulders with a cat o' nine tails or a chain studded with razor blades.

"There was so much blood flowing in the streets that it stank," the photographer told me. "I didn't know that human blood stank," I replied. "If there's enough of it, it does."

It should be mentioned that practices such as flagellation as part of a religious rite are not limited to Shia Islam. Modern processions of hooded flagellants during Lent are still a feature of certain Catholic countries such as Spain and self-flagellation is practiced by Catholics in the Philippines, Spain, Portugal and Italy and some of the countries in Latin America.

Most non-Muslims, along with Sunni Muslims and even some Shia Muslims, find this bloodletting the height of barbarity and apostasy. Some progressive-minded Shia men now use the occasion of Ashura to visit a blood bank and donate blood, a far more humane and socially-acceptable method of "sacrificing one's blood for the martyred Imam Hussein" than the public bloodletting that squanders blood into the gutter.

From a Sunni perspective, the cult of Hussein diverts the attention of the faithful from the Prophet Mohammed himself, sets up Hussein as something of a rival to Mohammed, and comes close to idolatry or polytheism.

In Saudi Arabia, the Ashura rituals were banned and repressed for decades and those brazen or foolhardy enough to perform self-mutilation publicly in Shia strongholds such as Qatif were subject to arrest. In Bahrain, too, for many years, the Government tried to prevent many of the Ashura processions and jailed participants. The Bahraini government no longer hinders these processions, and, according to press reports, in Saudi Arabia, Ashura processions in public are now permitted in Qatif, but still prohibited in the nearby cities of Dammam and Al Khobar.

Despite the periodic outbreaks of street demonstrations and repression, generally speaking, Bahrainis tend to be quite tolerant of religious differences. Shia and Sunni Muslims co-exist peacefully with each other and with Christians—both Arab and expatriate—Jews and Hindus. Shia religious holidays were officially recognized by the Bahraini government and the training courses were suspended on those days. As mentioned previously, King Hamad has even gone so far as to appoint a Jewish woman, Houda Ezra Nonoo, as the kingdom's ambassador in Washington, DC.

I was able to attend an Ashura street procession in the village of A'Ali, along with a colleague. Out of respect, we donned black trousers and shirts. No sooner had we arrived in the village than we were befriended by a young man, Sayeed, who spoke fluent English and, we learned, worked in a bank. He immediately volunteered to serve as our guide, escorting us along the route of the procession and explaining many of the details that would have otherwise escaped us.

We witnessed a reënactment of episodes in the Battle of Karbala. Umayyad soldiers—all dressed in garish red costumes and made up in scraggly beards, wigs and blackface—flogged Hussein mercilessly as he tumbled to the ground. Another frightening character threatened groups of children, representing those captured by King Yazid's army, with terrifying imprecations amplified and broadcast over a portable loudspeaker system. A cohort of men from a neighboring village marched to the beat of a drum, rhythmically pounding their chests as a gesture of mourning. We spotted one of our trainees in the group and waved; he promptly stepped out of the procession and came to greet us before returning to join his fellows. Another group of men and boys—some of them appearing as young as four or five—wielded steel flails and struck their backs and shoulders in unison, but with their shirts on and no blades on the flails. No blood was shed. Sayeed pointed out two distinguished-looking men, recently-elected members of the Bahraini parliament, carrying copies of the Quran as they marched. Parents hoisted their children, one after another, onto the backs of two placid camels. Other marchers, also costumed as Umayyad soldiers, waved blood-stained papier-mâché heads impaled on long pikes, symbolizing the beheaded Hussein and his companions. Many residents of A'Ali had set up stands or tables outside their homes offering free refreshments—food and drink—to participants and spectators alike.

This Ashura procession brought to my mind the medieval miracle plays, pageants also performed outdoors at Christmas or Easter. The Christian religious dramas reënacted episodes in the Passion of Jesus Christ, as symbolized in the Stations of the Cross found in many Catholic churches

Christianity has a martyr, too; Jesus Christ is martyred on the cross. But Christians believe that Jesus Christ is resurrected from the dead as part of a plan of salvation and redemption. There is no resurrection for the martyr in Shia Islam—the only icon is that of the bloody, dismembered corpse.

It seems to me that, conceivably, the origins of the sanguinary Ashura rituals—the flagellation and the self-mutilation—might go back in history not just to the seventh-century Battle of Karbala, but even further. A correspondent who lives on Cyprus reminded me that self-flagellation was practiced in most early civilizations, including Greece, Egypt and Mesopotamia. Isn't it therefore possible that these contemporary rites and rituals are the replications of ancient rites and rituals that may have been practiced by the inhabitants of Dilmun, the distant ancestors of today's Bahrainis? Might the streets of ancient Saar have once flowed with the blood of celebrants evoking the sufferings of some now-forgotten martyr in the pantheon of Dilmun's gods?

Thobes, Bishts, Uniforms and Shirts

The *thobe* is the ankle-length, long-sleeved, high-necked garment that is worn as national dress by many if not most men in the Gulf countries, including Bahrain. Summer *thobes* are white and made of cotton or polyester and winter *thobes* are fashioned from black, brown, grey or tan wool. They're usually sewn by tailors from India or Pakistan who specialize in producing these garments.

Along with the *thobe*, men wear a crocheted white skull cap known in Bahrain as a *keffiyeh* or *taqiyah*, covered by a large, square kerchief known as a *ghutra*—either pure white or red and white checked—folded in a triangle. There is no significance placed on which kind the man wears, although I tend to think that the white *ghutra* is more citified and the checked *ghutra* more traditional—more Bedouin.

The original purpose of the *ghutra* was functional: it was supposed to be wrapped around the face during desert storms to filter out the dust and sand. The *agal* is a thick, double, black cord that is worn on the top of the *ghutra* like a halo to hold it in place.

Particularly religious men in Saudi Arabia, such as the *mutaween* can easily be identified because they tend to have long beards and wear their *thobes* shorter—to mid-calf—following the example of the Prophet Mohammed, who they believe wore his *thobes* hemmed above the ankles.

Recently, the traditional *thobe* has claimed a place in the world of high fashion. According to an article that appeared in the English-language Saudi daily

Arab News, the Lomar factory near Jeddah is "redefining the *thobe* as a [sic] stylish attire than can be worn both as a fashion statement and as a statement of national pride." Lomar owners Loai Naseem and his wife Mona Haddad have employed 120 expatriate seamstresses and 15 Saudi women tailors to turn out 300 *thobes* a day in their four-million-dollar facility.[15]

For formal occasions, such as weddings, Bahraini men don their *bisht* over their thobe. A *bisht* is a heavy cloak made of wool, usually dyed black, brown, or grey, and trimmed in gold or silver embroidery. Unlike in the West, where you can rent black tie for a wedding, in Bahrain you have to buy your own *bisht*.

I had a conversation one day with one of the few trainees who always wore full national dress—*thobe, keffiyeh, ghutra* and *agal*. He explained to me that each of the Gulf nations has its own particular style of *thobe*.

Thus, there's a Saudi style, a Bahraini style, an Emirati style, a Qatari style and so on. The Qatari *thobe* is supposed to be the most stylish and elegant, so I asked him if he could provide me with the address of a tailor in Manama who could produce a Qatari *thobe* for me before I left Bahrain.

---

[15] "Thobes Enter a Stylish Era." *Arab News*, October 27, 2010.

My trainee also told me that prices for a *bisht* range upwards from 200 Bahraini dinars ($530.00 or €400.00) for the cheapest ones. I promptly decided that purchasing a *bisht* was a luxury that I could forego.

One morning a tailor and his assistant arrived at the training center and measured all the trainees for their uniforms. A few weeks later the uniforms arrived in several large cardboard boxes. Each trainee received a plastic bag containing two pairs of navy-blue trousers and two white shirts adorned with the logo of the training center embroidered in blue on the breast pocket.

The trainees were expected to purchase their own matching neckties and a pair of black shoes. I mentioned to some of them that they might like to check out the ties in the Mega Mart where I had bought some snazzy ones for a few dinars each. When the trainees arrived the next day, their appearance had greatly improved.

The trainees ranged in age from their late teens to their late twenties. Before receiving their uniforms, the dress code at the training center was pretty casual. Most of the trainees—except the handful who always looked sharp in their *thobes*—were outfitted in various types of Western attire. A few were dressed pretty shabbily, wearing cheap flip-flops instead of the traditional sandals and gaudy knee-length cut-offs or knock-off dungarees. Some sported faded tee-shirts, often adorned with a slogan in either misspelled or cryptic English.

For example, one trainee showed up one day wearing a tee-shirt boldly imprinted with FCUK. Did he know that "FCUK" is the name of a trendy British casual wear chain, French Connection United Kingdom? Did he have any notion of the significance of the intentional misspelling? My guess was that he had probably just bought it from a street vendor in the souk for a few hundred fils.

A couple of trainees asked me for help in tying their neckties; I was glad to give them personalized instructions in how to tie a Windsor knot, just as I had learned to tie it from my own father when I was a boy. I told one of the trainees that, one of these days, he would probably be teaching his son how to tie a Windsor knot just as I had taught him.

During the tailor's visit to the training center, I had taken advantage of the occasion to ask him if I could order some dress shirts. Of course, he was eager to accommodate a new customer. He promptly took my measurements and allowed me to pick the materials I wanted from the swatches in his sample book.

A few days later I took delivery of my tailor-made dress shirts acquired for the modest sum of 7 Bahraini dinars ($18.58 or €14.00) each. For comparison, fourteen euros is about what the seamstress in my neighborhood in Paris would charge me just to hem a pair of trousers. I told the tailor the only thing missing was a label sewn inside the collar declaring *Custom Tailored by A'Az al-Awttan of Manama*. Wouldn't that have been just as impressive as the label of a bespoke tailor on Savile Row or Jermyn Street?

Qatar

Since I was nearing the end of my three-month stay, I needed to make a quick trip out of the country to obtain a new stamp in my passport. The closest neighbor to Bahrain is Saudi Arabia, just 25 kilometers away on the other side of the causeway, but the Saudis do not issue individual tourist visas; the only way you can enter the Kingdom of the al Sauds on your own is on business or on pilgrimage. So, instead of crossing the bridge, I planned to fly the short hop to Doha, the capital of the State of Qatar.

Within a few years, however, people should have the option of zipping between Bahrain and Qatar by either driving or riding a high-speed train. A new causeway, the Qatar-Bahrain Friendship Bridge, stretching the 40 kilometers (24.85 miles) over the Gulf of Bahrain that separates the two countries, has been in the planning stages since 2008, but subject to numerous delays. In December 2012, Bahrain's Foreign Minister, Khalid bin Ahmed Al Khalifa, announced that construction was expected to be completed "a little before the 2022 FIFA World Cup matches," scheduled to be held in Qatar. If and when the project is realized, the structure will be the longest fixed link in the world. The cost was originally estimated at $5 billion.

Friendship is, indeed, the key, since the two countries—or rather, the two ruling clans, the Al Khalifas of Bahrain and the Al Thanis of Qatar—have been squabbling for centuries over disputed real estate, primarily the sparsely-inhabited Hawar Islands claimed by both countries, and an abandoned townsite in a small enclave called Zubara on the Qatari coast, claimed by Bahrain.

In 1986 the countries came to close to war when shots were fired by Qatari gunboats after Bahrain started to build up a disputed man-made reef called Fasht al Dibal, and Qatari soldiers captured several prisoners. Finally, in 1991, the case was brought before the World Court in The Hague. Ten years later—the case was the longest in the Court's history—a decision worthy of Solomon was reached granting Bahrain the Hawar Islands but ruling out their claim to any part of the Qatari peninsula.

My flight was scheduled for a Saturday, one of my days off. I was traveling with one of my colleagues and his wife; they planned to stay overnight in order to sightsee in Doha. When I woke up on Saturday morning I checked the weather and discovered that it was raining in Doha. I decided to don my trench coat for the first time since my arrival on October 24. That proved to be a wise decision.

When we got to the airport, my friends headed for a coffee shop for breakfast and I checked out the shops. I stopped by a tiny stall identified as "Bahraini Productive Families." I spotted several hand-woven baskets of the type I had bought in Bahrain during my first visit in the late 1970's. I talked with the woman in charge of the stall and asked her to show me some of the handicrafts she had for sale. She showed me more baskets—woven from date palm fronds—wooden jewel boxes and small jars filled with aromatic wood for use in incense burners. I asked the vendor to explain how the arts and crafts system worked. She answered that most of the articles are crafted by women in their homes. The government, through the Ministry of Social Development, then purchases these articles and sells them at locations such as this shop at the airport as well as a handicrafts center located in Al Jasra house, the birthplace of the former ruler, Isa bin Salman, located not far from the access ramp to the causeway. I told the saleswoman that I intended to buy some Bahraini handicrafts to take back as gifts and souvenirs. I couldn't resist buying a small basket since it only cost one Bahraini dinar.

The flight on Qatar Airways only took 25 minutes. In its television commercials, Qatar Airways boasts that it is "the world's 5-star airline," but I had to wonder who granted such a title and on what basis. At any rate, there wasn't much on such a short flight to judge the accuracy of the slogan, since as soon as we had been served plastic cups of orange juice, the pilot began his descent to Doha.

The population of Qatar (pronounced halfway between "cutter" and "gutter") is only 840,926 (2010 estimate), yet the country lies on the world's third largest reserves of natural gas, after those of Russia and Iran. Qatar's proven natural gas reserves stood at 910.5 trillion cubic feet as of January 2007, about 15 percent of the world total. With so few people and so much wealth, it is not surprising that Qatar's annual GNP per capita of around $100,000.00 is the highest in the world.

As we disembarked, I got the impression that we had flown to London instead of Doha. The sky was overcast, a chilly wind was blowing off the Gulf and light rain was falling. I was glad I was wearing my trench coat.

After I cleared customs, I headed for the immigration desk and handed over my passport to two Qatari women wearing *abayas* who did not stop gossiping except for one brief moment, when one of them paused long enough to ask, "Do you have a visa?" "No." "Then you have to pay." It turned out that "having to pay" cost me 100 Qatari riyals ($27.46 or €20.10). Ouch! I thought the Qataris were so rich with natural gas money that there should be no reason to charge visitors anything just to stamp a passport. But when I thumbed through my passport and finally located the Qatari stamp, I learned that I was also entitled to visit the Sultanate of Oman. Two countries for the price of one—now that was a bargain!

In the terminal building was a line of booths from the various hotels in Doha. My friends understood that reservations had been made at the Mercure and we expected that the hotel would run a shuttle bus. We found the Mercure booth, but nobody was manning it. At the same time, a couple of young men showed up at the booth; they were staying at the Mercure, too. We explained the situation to the employee at one of the adjacent booths, who suggested that we go outside to see if we could locate the shuttle bus since it came by every fifteen minutes or so. We didn't see any Mercure buses, but we did find the driver of another hotel bus who offered to drive us to the Mercure—for a price.

As we waited in the gloomy weather, we struck up a conversation with our new acquaintances. They were Jordanians who owned and operated a business importing cosmetics into Saudi Arabia, and were based in Dammam. They had come to Doha to attend the Asian Cup soccer match between Jordan and Kazakhstan and root for their team. My friends and I are familiar with the technique of creative visualization, so we assured the Jordanians that we would visualize a stunning victory for their glorious and talented team over the ignoble and brutish Uzbeks. I found out later that the Jordanians' enthusiasm and our visualization had come to naught: Jordan lost to Uzbekistan 2-1.

Knowing how many Saudi ladies pride themselves on their beauty, I suggested that their business must be very lucrative. The more talkative of the pair, identified on his business card as the Marketing Manager, confirmed my opinion about Saudi ladies, but cautioned that doing business in the Kingdom was fraught with many administrative hurdles—often unexpected or frivolous. In one example, the firm was compelled to withdraw a lipstick from the shelves because a Saudi bureaucrat had disapproved of its name (it was something like "Girl Friend"), declaring it too suggestive. "What are you going to do when you have to re-label 30,000 lipsticks?"

I suggested that the two partners might want to simplify their administrative problems by relocating their headquarters over the causeway in "Business-Friendly Bahrain" and commute every day like many of my former colleagues who worked at Saudi Aramco.

Tired of waiting for the Murcure shuttle bus to appear, we decided to accept the friendly driver's offer. We promptly clambered into the minibus and started haggling about the price, as is customary in the Middle East. Negotiations were particularly prickly since my friends were the only ones who had had the foresight to bring some Qatari riyals with them and, obviously, they didn't want to pay everybody's fare. The Jordanians had only brought Saudi riyals and I only had Bahraini dinars. I got out my smartphone and punched in the currency converter to help. The colloquy finally ended successfully, with each of us handing the driver the agreed-upon amounts of cash and all sides believing that they had gotten the best of the bargain. I have read that Saudi Arabia, Bahrain, the Emirates, and Qatar have plans to create a common currency, a Gulf dinar. It may be a gain for efficiency, but it will sound the death knell for the ancient and honorable custom of haggling.

When we arrived at the Mercure, it transpired that no reservations had been made. My friends were able to secure a room and decided to stay the night so they could discover the sights of Doha. I was so discouraged by the bad weather that I decided to take a taxi back to the airport and catch the afternoon flight at 4:45. In the meantime, the three of us had time to enjoy a tasty and copious buffet lunch at the hotel, and we were even able to order wine and beer to accompany our food. It seems that Qatar is like Bahrain in that alcoholic beverages can legally be sold in hotels and restaurants catering to a non-Muslim clientele.

On the way to the airport, the taxi drove through streets lined with modest one- or two-story buildings, small shops and restaurants. One shop in particular caught my eye: a large signboard proclaimed the establishment to be the "Qatar National Library." I surmised that the owner had confused "bookstore" with "library." It wouldn't be the first time: in French, the word for "bookstore" is *librairie,* but the word for "library" is *bibliothèque.* I reasoned that, if there was a Qatar National Library, it would be located in a more prestigious location and in more distinguished premises.

After my return to Bahrain I ran an internet search for "Qatar National Library" and discovered, not to my surprise, that a futuristic-looking 13-story building of that name, designed by the award-winning architect Arata Isozaki, was due for construction on the prestigious Doha Corniche.

As I was wandering around the terminal trying to find my departure gate, I almost collided with a colossal, grey automobile parked right in the middle of the departure lounge. A sign identified it as a Rolls Royce Ghost. It looked as big as a Sherman tank. (Riddle: What's the difference between a

Rolls-Royce and a Bentley?[16] Answer: the owner drives a Bentley, but in a Rolls Royce the owner is driven.)

I wondered what this monstrosity was doing in the middle of an airport departure lounge. Then I spotted nearby a booth staffed by a pair of attractive young women whom I took to be Filipinas. "Do you want to try your luck today, sir?" cajoled one of them with a big smile. It appeared that the stand was operated by Qatar Duty Free (QDF), and the Ghost was being raffled off. A signboard behind the stand announced that the prizes not only included the Ghost, but also a Lexus IS 300 C and, the biggest prize of all, "ONE MILLION US DOLLAR" [sic]. Since there's no room to park a Sherman tank–or even a Lexus—on the street where I live, the only raffle that really attracted my attention was for the million dollars. Tickets were priced in Qatari and United States currency. Taking a chance on the million-dollar prize cost $263 (€193). I thought about all the money I had lost in the stock market over past decades and thought that losing an additional $263 wouldn't hurt that much. But then on the other hand, I pulled out my smartphone, divided a million by 263 and determined that they would have to sell at least 3,802 tickets just to break even. And since QDF was a profit-making

---

[16] From the end of World War II until the company split and Bentley was bought by Volkswagen, the two cars were both made by Rolls Royce and were virtually identical except for their grilles and hood ornaments. Advertisements recommended the slightly less-expensive Bentley for those customers who were "diffident" about buying a showier Rolls-Royce.

organization and had to pay salaries to those Filipinas and meet all the other expenses required to run a business, I wondered how many tickets were actually sold. I subsequently went onto the internet and learned that QDF sells 5,000 tickets for each million-dollar prize, thereby netting a gross profit of $315,000 for each contest. Not a bad take for a raffle! I concluded that the real way to make a million dollars on one of these raffles was by organizing and sponsoring it, not by playing it. In Qatar, as in Las Vegas, the House always wins.

What would you have done?

The Wrap-up

With my departure date less than a fortnight away, my winter in the middle of two seas was drawing to a close.

I decided to set down some final impressions before leaving Bahrain.

Christianity in Bahrain

In a conversation with a Bahraini manager, the subject or religious tolerance came up. After some discussion and research, I learned that, not only are there several Christian churches in Bahrain today, but the historic presence of Christianity on the island dates back to the first centuries of the faith's existence. I discovered that during the 3rd or 4th centuries AD, many inhabitants of Bahrain appear to have adopted Christianity. It is documented that the Nestorian denomination of Christianity was well-established in Bahrain and on the Arabian Peninsula by the early 5th century. Bahrain remained a center of Christianity until adopting Islam in 629 AD. Furthermore, the names of several villages on Bahrain's Muharraq Island reflect this Christian legacy; the name of one village, Al Dair, for example, means "the monastery."

On the Saudi side of the Gulf and up the coast near the town of Jubail lie the ruins of a Nestorian church, estimated to date from the 4th century, making it older than any known Christian church in Europe. For comparison, the oldest church building in France is the basilica of Saint-Pierre-aux-Nonnains in Metz. The building was originally erected in 380

AD as part of a Roman spa complex, but was not converted into use as a church until the 7th century.

How They Knew I Had Lived in Saudi Arabia

Although I never formally studied Arabic, it was inevitable that I would pick up at least a working vocabulary of common phrases and expressions of the colloquial Gulf Arabic dialect when I was in Saudi Arabia. I remember being told at the time that, although Bahrain was just 25 kilometers away, the dialect they spoke there was different.

One day when it rained, I mentioned to the trainees that it was *moya*, which is the word Saudis use for "water." But one of the trainees replied, "That's how the Saudis say it; we say *miya*." Another example occurred when the term "spark plug" came up in one of the lessons. Knowing that, in Saudi Arabia, they use the French word, *bougie*, I suggested this as the appropriate Arabic translation. Wrong again: in Bahrain, they've adopted a modified form of the English word "plug." When a Bahraini says it, it sounds like a cross between "blog" and "block." So, even if I had not told the trainees at the beginning of the course that I had lived in Saudi Arabia, they would have discovered it on their own. It reminded me of the Biblical story of *shibboleth* and *sibboleth*, but with less sanguinary consequences: as recounted in the twelfth chapter of the Book of Judges, two and forty thousand Ephraimites were slain because they couldn't pronounce *shibboleth* correctly!

Gifts

Arab generosity is legendary, and I was very touched by some of the gifts I received from the trainees. Several performed the pilgrimage to Mecca during the Hajj season. One of them, who had made the pilgrimage to pray for his grandfather, presented me with a chaplet of prayer beads that he had brought back from Islam's holiest shrine.

Looking very much like a Catholic rosary, the chaplet consists of three sections of round beads carved from olive wood, two sections of thirty-three beads and one of thirty-four. When you add them up you get 100, one for each of the ninety-nine attributes of God, and the hundredth representing the highest name, the Arabic word for God Almighty, *Allah*.

Whereas in Islam there are 99 words for God, by contrast, in Judaism, the name of God is considered so sacred that, for some Jews it is ineffable, and many Jews will write the word as "G-d."

Another trainee, who had also made the hajj pilgrimage, brought me a bottle of water from the Zamzam well in Mecca. Like the water in many other springs around the world, Zamzam water is considered by many to possess curative properties.

According to Islamic belief, Zamzam is a miraculously-generated source of water from God, which first flowed thousands of years ago when Abraham's son Ishmael was thirsty and kept crying for water. As he kicked the ground, water gushed out. Millions visit the well each year while performing the hajj or umrah[17] pilgrimages in order to drink its water.

A Shia trainee, who had made the pilgrimage to their holy city of Karbala in Iraq for the Ashura ceremonies, presented me with a *turba*. This consists of a lump of the clayey soil found at Karbala compressed into a small, flat cylinder and inscribed with the name of God in Arabic. Practitioners of Shia Islam believe that when they prostrate themselves in their daily prayers, their forehead should touch natural soil, not a man-made prayer rug, and the most favored soil is that of Karbala, the site of the martyrdom of Imam Al Hussein, shaped into a *turba*. To Sunnis, of course, the *turba* is just one more symbol of the Shias' idolatry. The wife of a colleague of mine even had a *turba* confiscated by Saudi customs officials.

My Qatari Thobe

Following my trainee's instructions, I was fitted for my Qatari-style *thobe* and picked it up at the tailor's shop a few days afterwards. I had been told that the fair price would be between 11 and 14 Bahraini dinars and that I shouldn't pay one fils more; in point of fact, it cost me 12 dinars. I also purchased the requisite undergarment, a calf-length pair of baggy, cotton drawers known as *serwal*. That cost one additional dinar. To complete my sartorial outfit,

---

[17] Umrah is a pilgrimage to Mecca performed any time of the year. Hajj is only performed during the month of Dhu al Hijja

my trainee kindly offered me a set of cufflinks; *thobes* are fitted with French cuffs, and he wanted to be sure that I would be able to fasten them properly.

After the end of classes, one of my colleagues—who had also received numerous gifts—and I decided to issue an open invitation; if any of the trainees would like to meet with us informally, they could join us at one of the coffee shops on the Strip on Thursday morning. About half a dozen showed up. Since we had issued the invitation, my colleague and I thought it appropriate that we treat our guests to refreshments. Despite our protestations, they would hear none of it and insisted firmly that they would treat us: we were their guests in their country and the laws of Arab hospitality prevail.

Fijeri

When my friends and I had visited the National Museum, one of the most impressive exhibits was a full-scale model of a pearl-fishing boat accompanied by explanatory panels and showcases. One item on display was a paymaster's record of the job titles and respective wages of the members of the crew, one of whom was identified as a "singer." I wondered why the pearl-divers needed a singer on board, so I decided to follow it up with my Bahraini acquaintances. What I discovered was that there was a whole repertory of vocal music known as *fijeri*, a type of sea chantey that was sung by the pearl divers of Bahrain, Kuwait and Qatar—who often spent many months at sea—as a way to relieve the boredom and loneliness of their long peregrinations away from home.

When researching *fijeri* on the internet I came across a video clip of a live performance. The lead singer accompanied himself on the oud—the Arabian ancestor of our lute, but tuned in quarter-tones—supported by a chorus of singers and musicians playing a small double-sided hand-drum, known as the *mirwas,* and the *jahlah*, a clay pot played with both hands. After each of the lead singer's solos, the chorus would respond with sophisticated, polyrhythmic handclapping. This call-and-response suggested an African origin of *fijeri,* which one of my Bahraini colleagues, an oud-player himself, confirmed.

The Gulf's First Oil Well

One weekend, two of my colleagues and I decided to visit Bahrain's first oil well and the Dar al Naft, the Bahrain Oil Museum, located in the center of the island. Although the museum was closed, we were able to inspect the well. Jabal al Dukhan No. 1 was spudded in on October 16, 1931, and struck oil on June 1, 1932. It was the first producing oil well in the entire Gulf region—oil would not flow from Saudi Arabia's first producing well, Dammam No. 7, until 1938.

To me, this was the quintessential symbol of the unimaginable wealth and consequent economic development made possible by the production and export of petroleum by Bahrain and its Gulf neighbors. It all started here.

The iconic well is no longer in production, but it has been preserved *in situ* next to the museum. Although Bahrain's oil production today is infinitesimal compared to that of neighboring Saudi Arabia, modern recovery techniques and a price in the neighborhood of $100 a barrel have encouraged the Bahrainis to drill new wells. One such well, located just up the hill, not far from Jabal al Dukhan No. 1, was brought into production early in 2010.

Camping in the Desert

On our way to visit Jabal al Dukhan No. 1, we drove through a desert area known as the Sakhir, dotted on either side of the road with innumerable large-size, canvas tents. At first we thought the tents were used to house the oil workers, since producing wells, rhythmically pumping their black gold, were scattered on both sides of the highway, but we subsequently learned that these tents served another purpose entirely.

In the winter months, particularly between December and April, many Bahraini families escape urban life during the weekends and school holidays to renew their traditional lifestyle by camping in the desert. Families buy or rent their tents and assure privacy by locating them behind mesh fences made of reeds or palm fronds. The tents and common areas are located inside.

The special nature of camping in the Bahrain wilderness is about families gathering in one place, enjoying the cool weather, sitting to chat and sharing food and drink. Storytellers recount the lives of their ancestors, many of whom lived the same way. The difference is that camping has become a luxury when in the past it was the way of life for many.

Although for most non-Bahrainis, the idea of "camping in the desert" means living simply and renouncing modern conveniences, Bahrainis prefer to bring the conveniences with them. Tents have become similar to complete houses. They are now equipped with televisions, satellite dishes and DVD players in addition to gas ovens for cooking and other household appliances. Inside, colorful fabrics are often used to decorate the walls, and carpets cover the sandy floor.

A Delicate Balance

A quick look at the map reveals that the small island kingdom of Bahrain is located at the heart of the strategically important Gulf. Oil-rich Saudi Arabia, natural gas-rich Qatar and Iran, with seventy million inhabitants, all lie within close proximity of Bahrain's shores.

The delicate balancing act required of the Al Khalifa monarchy is how to maintain the precarious equilibrium between the powerful Sunnis of Saudi Arabia and the equally powerful Shias of Iran, a task rendered even more difficult since Shias compose a majority of the Bahraini population although, as

Justin Gengler has demonstrated, that percentage is less than 60% and is steadily declining.

The Saudis generously subsidize Bahrain—they financed the entire cost of the causeway linking the two countries—because they would prefer that the Al Khalifas keep the Shias under control on their side of the causeway than deal with a potentially restive Shia minority of their own.

On the north shore of the Gulf, the Shia mullahs and ayatollahs of the Iranian theocracy enviously eye the islands of Bahrain, which were under Persian suzerainty between 1602 and 1717.

In November 1957, Iran's parliament passed a bill declaring Bahrain to be Iran's fourteenth province, and allocated two empty seats for its representatives.

This claim appears to have been renewed recently. According to one of the released WikiLeaks cables, in March 2009, **Ali Akbar Nateq Nura, an advisor to Iran's Supreme Leader, again** referred to Bahrain as Iran's fourteenth province.

The Iranians would like nothing better than to extend their strategic reach into Bahrain and, to that end, maintain contacts with and exert influence over radical Shia groups within Bahrain. The Saudis are just as determined to prevent this Iranian *Anschluss*. The Saudis' worst nightmare would be a Shia takeover of Bahrain, an "Iranization" that would be followed by an extension of the contagion into the Shia-majority areas of the **Eastern Province** of Saudi Arabia around Qatif, Dammam and Hofuf, where most of the oil fields are located. In mid-2012, street protests did occur in Qatif; police intervened and made a number of arrests.

And then, there's the role of the United States. Bahrain has been host to the United States Navy for over sixty years, and a defense pact signed in 1991 designated Bahrain as a "major non-NATO ally." Only a short distance from my residence in the Juffair neighborhood of Manama lies the Naval Support Activity Bahrain (NSA Bahrain), home of the U.S. Naval Forces Central Command and the United States Fifth Fleet. The goal of this facility is to maintain political stability and the free flow of oil to the global economy.

These are all players on the multi-dimensional geopolitical chessboard of the Middle East, and the role of tiny Bahrain in this game is much more than that of a mere pawn.

The Truth about Bahrain

A few hours after I left Bahrain, on the morning of February 14, 2011—Valentine's Day—groups of Shia militants demonstrated in the heart of the island's capital, Manama. What for some was a Day of Love, for others was a Day of Rage.

The events that ensued have continued into mid-2013. Although I provided in the previous chapter an overview of the delicate political balance required of the Al Khalifa monarchy, recent events in the island kingdom lead me to offer a more detailed, historical analysis of the geopolitical situation in Bahrain.

First of all, sectarian unrest in Bahrain is nothing new. Revolts and protests of the Shias against the ruling Sunnis have been breaking out periodically for decades and are always suppressed with a heavy hand. In fact, some of the previous uprisings were even more violent than the recent events and persisted for many years.

The wave of Shia protests against the government actually began over thirty years ago in the aftermath of the Iranian Revolution of 1979. The Ayatollah Khomeini and the Shia mullahs in Tehran viewed their co-religionists in Bahrain as potential agents and allies in their policy of exporting revolution among Shia dissidents across the Middle East.

In an article published in the *Wall Street Journal* on October 6, 2011, Mitchell A. Belfer wrote, "Since Iran's 1979 revolution, the country's leaders have assumed that their revolution represents the aspirations of Shiites throughout the Mideast. That is why they have worked to undermine the Sunni Khalifa family's legitimacy in Bahrain by promoting an ideology of Shiite empowerment."

In 1981, an Islamic Front for the Liberation of Bahrain, aided and abetted by Iran, attempted a coup d'état in Bahrain with the view of overthrowing the monarchy and assassinating the Bahraini leadership.

The plotters wanted to establish a theocratic system based on the Iranian model, with Shia control of the government and a local Shia cleric as Supreme Leader of the theocracy.

The coup, however, was detected and thwarted thanks to a tip-off from a "friendly intelligence source."

One of the consequences of the attempted coup was the formation of the Gulf Cooperation Council or GCC, which Bahrain joined along with Kuwait, Oman, Qatar, Saudi Arabia and the United Arab Emirates. Thus, it was under the ægis of the GCC that troops from Saudi Arabia crossed the causeway to defend vital government and commercial installations and essential infrastructure during the 2011 uprising.

Shia frustration over the lack of a fully representative democracy led to new protests that began on December 17, 1994, and continued for over six years. Opponents of the monarchy rioted, bombs were set off and the police responded with brutal tactics identical to those that have been employed since February 2011. More than forty people were killed during these events.

Bahrain had promulgated its first constitution in 1973, establishing an elected parliament. But only one parliamentary election was held, and Isa bin Salman Al Khalifa abrogated the constitution in 1975. Bahrain was governed under emergency laws from 1975 to 2002.

In 1999 Hamad bin Isa Al Khalifa assumed the throne after the death of his father and began to implement social and political reforms. He abolished security laws and released jailed dissidents.

Hamad viewed himself as a reformer and drew up a National Action Charter, incorporating a new constitution with provisions for a bicameral parliament and universal suffrage. A referendum on the charter was held on February 14-15, 2002, and approved by 98.4% of the voters.

In a television interview[18] on July 25, 2012, France 24 journalist Douglas Herbert asked Bahraini Foreign Minister, Khalid bin Ahmed Al Khalifa, if the Arab Spring was coming to Bahrain. The minister replied that it had started in Bahrain ten years ago, an obvious reference to the enactment of the constitution by the 2002 referendum.

---

[18] "The Interview," France 24, July 25, 2012.

The referendum brought an end to political violence, but did not initially bring about reconciliation between the government and most of the opposition groups who considered the changes largely superficial.

Shia street protests began once again in August 2010 and, once again, the protests were met with a harsh crackdown and accusations by the government that the protestors were attempting another coup d'état. More than 350 demonstrators and militants were arrested.

Although it escaped the attention of the outside world at the time, Bahraini police opened fire on Shia Muslims at mourning ceremonies on December 11, 2010, a few days before Ashura, in the fishing village of Malkiya, on the west coast of the island, one of several Shia villages that have seen unrest since late 2007. Clashes erupted when police tried to remove black flags hoisted by Shias as a sign of mourning. According to one press account,[19] the attack injured three men.

The February 14, 2011, protest started peacefully, with Shia demonstrators congregating in the Pearl Roundabout traffic circle in the heart of Manama. But the Bahraini security forces launched a violent attack on the protestors and at least two were killed.

---

[19] "Three injured in clashes between Shias and police in Bahrain," reprinted from Deutsche Press-Agentur on MonstersandCritics.com, December 11, 2010.

A few days later, the security forces launched another furious attack in the middle of the night, tear-gassing the mostly-sleeping demonstrators and peppering them with bird shot and rubber-coated bullets. Many were injured and a number were killed by shots fired at close range.

To further complicate matters, Shias are largely excluded from the police force and from the military. Some have claimed that the Bahraini riot police force is mostly made up of non-native Bahrainis. According to Steven Sotloff, a fellow at the Washington DC-based Foundation for Defense of Democracies, "They are foreign Sunnis from Pakistan, from Yemen and Jordan, they are beholden to their paymasters—the monarchy—not the citizenry...They [are granted Bahraini citizenship] on a fast-track, they are given affordable housing that Bahraini citizens do not get, and the grievances stem from this."[20]

Even more worrisome, the *Daily Telegraph*, in an article[21] dated February 18, 2010, quoted WikiLeaks cables in which King Hamad warned U.S. General David Petraeus in July 2008 that Bahraini opposition groups were being trained in Lebanon by Hezbollah and that Syria had provided them with fake passports. An American diplomat's analysis tended to dismiss these allegations. Yet, whether or not they

---

[20] "Big powers warily eye revolt in the world's smallest Arab nation." France24, February 11, 2011.

[21] Hope, Christopher, "WikiLeaks: Bahrain opposition 'received training from Hizbollah,'" *The Telegraph*, February 18, 2011.

are true, they help explain the thinking behind the violent repression of the Shia dissenters.

Whereas in the past western media had largely ignored civil dissent in Bahrain, in 2011, thanks to events in Tunisia and Egypt—and thanks to cell phones and social media—the whole world was watching the suppression of the Shia protestors, and most of the media coverage was highly unfavorable to the Al Khalifa monarchy. Even Secretary of State Hillary Clinton, who had praised Bahrain's parliamentary and municipal elections during her state visit to the nation on December 4, 2010, felt compelled to call the Bahraini Foreign Minister on March 19, 2011, and administer a stern dressing-down, expressing her "deep concern" at the violence of the repression.

As could be expected, however, most of the media, whose reporters have no background in or understanding of the socio-political complexity of Bahrain, got it wrong, erroneously comparing the events in Bahrain to the Arab Spring uprisings in Tunisia and Egypt.

Mitchell A. Belfer commented, "Thirty years of intransigence reveal the extent of Tehran's determination to turn Bahrain into an Iranian satellite. So Iran's machinations during this year's protests should have had the international community rushing to support Bahrain, not ostracize it."

Furthermore, Arabist Lee Smith, writing in the *Weekly Standard* on April 1, 2011, observed, [22] "Tehran sees the Shia largely as pawns to be used against their Saudi adversaries, as well as against Washington."

On February 16, 2011, I called one of my former trainees. He assured me that he and his family were safe and well and admonished me not to believe everything I saw on television. Coincidentally, his views were confirmed in an article[23] that appeared, the next day in the *New York Times* entitled, "Bahrain's Sunnis Defend Monarchy." The author, Michael Slackman, reporting from Manama, had interviewed four young professionals who supported the government.

"Whose fault is it when you have five or six kids and you can't afford two?" Ms. Mohammed, an art curator, asked. "Why is that the government's fault?"

"I don't want a democracy," said Rayyah Mohammed, 32, an art project director and strong supporter of King Hamad. "I want a monarchy. I like how things are. I have a job. I have a house. I have free health care."

With respect to the foreigners employed in the security forces, the group felt that a police force

---

[22] Smith, Lee. "Touring Bahrain," The Weekly Standard, April 1, 2011.

[23] Slackman, Michael, "Bahrain's Sunnis Defend Monarchy," *New York Times*, February 17, 2011.

staffed by foreigners was preferable to a police force staffed by Shia citizens. They also said they feared a Shia government might be too religious and impose restrictions on society.

Nevertheless, there can be no doubt that the Al Khalifas bungled and overreacted to the protests by employing uncalled-for violence against the peaceful demonstrators. They should have known that Shia Islam is a religion of martyrs: martyrdom is an integral part of the Shia belief system. So the hard-liners in the government played into the Shias' hands, and there are now many more martyrs to add to their hagiography.

In an attempt to enhance international recognition of Bahrain, as a spur to the local economy and as an incentive to international investment, the Bahraini government invested $150 million to construct the Bahrain International Circuit (BIC), which opened in 2004 and employs over 3,000 people during the automobile racing season. The BIC, located at Sakhir—30 kilometers south of Manama—is actually a complex incorporating six different tracks, including the Formula-1 circuit used for the annual Bahrain Grand Prix race.

The same day that two of my colleagues and I made a trip to Bahrain's first oil well at Jabal al Dukhan, we visited the BIC. We stopped by the pits, where visitors could enroll in a training session followed by laps around the circuit at the wheel of a Caterham G7, a scaled-down racing vehicle derived from the Lotus Seven and especially adapted for Bahrain's heat and humidity. We also rode the elevator to the top of the eight-story Sakhir Tower, where we could view the Caterhams buzzing noisily around the track and survey the surrounding countryside from the open-air observation deck.

The BIC was scheduled to host the first Formula One Grand Prix race of the season on March 13, 2011. However, due to the civil unrest, the race was cancelled.

The 2012 Formula One calendar scheduled a race in Bahrain for April 22, the fourth of the season. The international media were disappointed if they had expected the worst to happen. In what turned out to be a public relations victory for the Al Khalifas, the race went off without a hitch. It was won after 57 laps by Sebastian Vettel of Germany at the wheel of a Renault RS27 2.4V8.

In a nutshell, the crux of the discord in Bahrain is a battle between the Saudis and the Iranians to exert control over the strategically-situated archipelago: the Saudis have it; the Iranians want it.

On a larger scale, Iran produces around four million barrels of oil per day and Saudi Arabia around ten million barrels per day. In a worst-case scenario, were Tehran to succeed in gaining control over oil production in the Eastern Province of Saudi Arabia, Iran would become an economic superpower able to hold the rest of the world hostage.

Most of the media in the West tend to sympathize unquestioningly with the demands of the Shia protestors in Bahrain, totally unaware of the implications of the creation of an Iran-linked theocracy in Bahrain. However, the oil-importing nations in the West and in Asia have no choice but to support the Al Khalifas and use diplomatic means and persuasion to cajole them into improving the conditions of the Shia and integrating them more firmly into the social fabric of the country.

The Bahrainis themselves—both Sunni and Shia—are like conjoined twins, condemned to coexist together in the same space. The only solution to the current unrest is reconciliation, and the only path to reconciliation is recognition by everyone that all Bahrainis must be treated equally and enjoy equal rights and opportunities.

The aviation training program in which I participated was a project to integrate young Bahrainis,[24] mostly Shia, into the mainstream of society, and I consider the program highly successful. It is my hope that programs such as these can be considerably expanded and that the thousands of young Shias who have been demonstrating in the streets of their villages and neighborhoods can take their rightful place in Bahraini society and enjoy good education, good jobs, good housing and good health care.

There is a hopeful sign: on March 10, 2011, the GCC governments pledged $20 billion in financial assistance over 10 years to be split between Bahrain

---

[24] Out of a total of 120 trainees, four were women.

and Oman and used to implement job-creation programs in both countries.[25]

This is also what everyone in Bahrain wants. It is my hope that they achieve it.

---

[25] El-Tabliwy, Tarek, "GCC pledges $20 billion in aid for Oman, Bahrain," *Washington Post*, March 10, 2011.

Index

A

A'Ali 85, 86
A'Az al-Awttan 94
abaya 53, 54
Abd Al Wahhab, Mohammed 36
Abu Dhabi 22, 37
Ahmadiyya 49
Air Arabia 16
Al A'Ali Mall 63, 64
Al Dair 111
Al Jasra house 101
Al Jazeera 31
Al Jazira Mall 38
Al Khalifa. 15, 36, 52, 118, 123, 128
Al Khalifa, Abdullah bin Muhammed bin Rashid 55
Al Khalifa, Ahmad Al Fateh bin Muhammed 36
Al Khalifa, Hamad bin Isa 36, 50, 55, 85, 125, 127, 129
Al Khalifa, Isa bin Salman 101, 125
Al Khalifa, Khalid bin Ahmed 99, 125
Al Khalifa, Sheikha Haya Rashed 34
Al Khobar 22, 85

Al Qaoud, Latifa 35
Al Rifa 50
Al Saud, Abdulaziz ibn Abdul Rahman ibn Faisal 39, 58
Al Thani 36, 99
Al Wefaq 36
Alawites 49
alcohol ..24, 38, 39, 40, 57, 67, 68, 105
Aleppo soap 69
Arab Spring 125, 128
Arabian Gulf 14
Arabian Peninsula.. 22, 36, 44, 55, 62, 79, 111
Arabian Sands 62
Arabian Sea 44
Arabic ...15, 39, 45, 53, 62, 82, 112, 113, 114
Aramcon 39, 40
Ashraf 30
Ashura ..82, 83, 84, 85, 86, 87, 114, 126
Asir Province, Saudi Arabia 53, 65
Ayatollah Khomeini ... 123

B

Bahrain Air 16
Bahrain International Circuit 130

135

Bahrain World Trade Center 25
Bahraini dinar ... 16, 61, 68, 69, 93, 94, 104, 114
Barbar 79, 80
Bateel 63
Battle of Karbala 82, 85, 87
BBC 31, 75
Bedouins 62
Beer Drinkers 23, 45
Belfer, Mitchell A. 123, 128
Bibby, Geoffrey 23, 24, 79, 80
Blue Flame, The 39
Book of Judges 112
bottle shops 67, 68
Budaiya 37, 38, 50
Buraida, Saudi Arabia ... 58
Burj Khalifa 13
Business-Friendly Bahrain 29, 37, 104

C

camping 117, 118
Caterham 131
Catholicism 49, 51
Christian 36, 51, 52, 54, 86, 111
Clinton, Hillary 128
CNN 31, 75
Coachella Valley 63

Council of Representatives 33, 35, 36, 50

D

Dammam 55, 85, 103, 116, 119
Dates 62
Day of Rage 17
Dhahran 39, 40, 44
Dilmun .. 22, 23, 24, 43, 44, 45, 73, 79, 80, 87
Doha 99, 100, 101, 102, 103, 104
Dubai 13, 37, 38, 74

E

Eastern Province, Saudi Arabia .. 21, 49, 119, 131
Egypt 87, 128
Elections 34, 35, 36, 50, 128
Emirates Airlines 16
Empty Quarter 62
Etihad Airways 16

F

Fasht al Dibal 100
FCUK 94
FIFA World Cup 99
fijeri 115, 116
Formula One 131
Foundation for Defense of Democracies 127

France... 34, 44, 51, 67, 68, 69, 81, 111, 125
Friendship Bridge.... 15, 99

G

Gengler, Justin 49, 119
Girl Friend 103
Greece 44, 87
Gulf Air 16, 29
Gulf Cooperation Council
 124
Gulf of Bahrain 15, 99

H

hajj 113, 114
Hamad Town 50
hamour 39
Hawar Islands........ 99, 100
Hezbollah 127
Hofuf, ... 21, 119
House of Commons....... 33
House of Lords.............. 33
House of Saud 36
Hussein, Saddam 51

I

Indonesia 53
Iran 15, 49, 50, 51, 101, 118, 119, 123, 124, 128, 131, 132
Iran's fourteenth province
 119
Iraq . 14, 49, 50, 51, 54, 55, 62, 82, 114

Isa Town 50
Islam 51, 52, 53, 55, 56, 57, 84, 87, 111, 113, 114, 130
Islamic Front for the Liberation of Bahrain
 124
Islamic National Accord Association............... 36
Ismaila 49
Isozaki, Arata.............. 105

J

Jabal al Dukhan No. 1 116, 117
Jesus 87
Jewish (Bahraini)... 36, 55, 65, 85
Jordan 33, 54, 103, 127
Jubail 55, 111
Judaism 113
Juffair 31, 120

K

Karbala 114
Kazakhstan 103
Kentucky 24, 74
Kentucky, Commonwealth of 62
Khadouri, Nancy 36
King Fahd Causeway.... 15
Kuwait 14, 22, 33, 115, 124

L

Lamb, General Sir Graeme 34
Las Vegas 107
Levant 44, 79
Looking for Dilmun. 23, 45

M

Malkiya 126
Mall of America 64
Manama 21, 22, 25, 29, 55, 92, 94, 120, 123, 126, 129, 130
Mega Mart ... 61, 65, 68, 93
Middle East 35, 37, 63, 104, 120, 123, 141
Ministry of Social Development 101
Mohammed bin Saud 36
Mohammed III 37
Mohammed, Prophet 49, 51, 64, 82, 84, 91
Monaco 13
monarchy 33, 118, 123, 124, 127, 128, 129
Morocco, Kingdom of ... 37
Muharraq Island 50, 111
Muslims 24, 38, 49, 51, 54, 56, 57, 67, 82, 84, 85, 126

N

National Action Charter 125
National Assembly 33
National Museum ... 22, 43
Nestorian Christianity .. 55, 111
Nonoo, Houda Ezra 55, 85
Nura, Ali Akbar Nateq 119

O

Oman 14, 102, 124, 133
Oradour-sur-Glane .. 81, 82

P

Palestine 54
Petraeus, David 127
Protestantism 50

Q

Qarrisah, Hala 36
Qatar 14, 15, 31, 36, 97, 99, 101, 104, 105, 106, 115, 118, 124
Qatar Airways 16, 101
Qatar National Library 105
Qatif 23, 49, 84, 119
Quran 39, 52, 65, 86

R

Ramadan 57, 62
referendum 125, 126
Rolls Royce 105, 106

Roosevelt, Franklin D. ..13
Rose, Charlie 43

S

Saar 79, 81, 82, 87
Safwa 49
Saint-Pierre-aux-Nonnains
.... 111
Sakhir 117, 130, 131
Samaan, Alice Thomas
   Yusuf 55
Saudi Arabia 14, 15, 21, 24,
   25, 26, 27, 30, 33, 36,
   37, 38, 39, 40, 45, 49,
   52, 53, 54, 55, 56, 62,
   63, 64, 65, 67, 84, 91,
   99, 103, 104, 112, 116,
   117, 118, 119, 124, 131
Saudi Aramco 24, 104
schadenfreude 46
Seef Mall 24, 25, 26, 64
Sharjah 37
Shia 16, 17, 36, 49, 50, 51,
   52, 54, 56, 82, 83, 84,
   85, 87, 114, 119, 123,
   124, 126, 128, 129, 130,
   131, 132
shibboleth and *sibboleth*
.... 112
Shura Council 33, 36, 54
Sitra Peninsula 50
Slackman, Michael 129
Smith, Lee 129

Sotloff, Steven 127
Strip, the 61, 66, 73, 74,
   115
Sunni 49, 50, 51, 52, 56, 84,
   85, 124, 132
Switzerland 34
synagogue 55

T

Tamkeen 16
Tarut Island 23, 49
Tatton Brewery 23
Thesiger, Sir Wilfred 62
thobe 91, 92, 114
Treaty of Peace and
   Friendship 37
Tuaregs 54
Tunisia 128
turba 114

U

umrah 114
United Arab Emirates .. 13,
   14, 16, 33, 37, 124
United Kingdom 33, 45, 94
United Nations General
   Assembly 34
United States 37, 55, 57, 63,
   70, 120
United States Fifth Fleet
   120
United States Navy 120
Universal suffrage 125

V

veil 52, 53, 54
Vettel, Sebastian 131

W

WikiLeaks 119, 127
Windsor knot 94

World Court 100

Y

Yemen 53, 65, 127

Z

Zamzam 113
Zubara 100

About the Author

Ronald W. Kenyon was born and raised in Ashland, Kentucky. He graduated from the University of Michigan, Ann Arbor, where he specialized in English literature, political science, French and Spanish and was awarded Avery Hopwood awards in creative writing for poetry and drama. He completed his graduate studies at Stanford after receiving a Woodrow Wilson National Fellowship and at Saint Lawrence University under a National Defense Education Act scholarship. He was certified as a French-English liaison interpreter by the U.S. Department of State Office of Language Services.

Ronald W. Kenyon spent ten years living and working in the Middle East, and has researched the region extensively. Aside from Bahrain, he has visited 47 countries in the Americas, Europe, Asia and Africa.

Since 2012, he has published collections of poetry and essays as well as a biography in English and French of an eighteenth-century French aristocrat, François Racine de Monville, and five albums of color photography.

In January 1980, he was chief photographer for a project to document traditional architecture in Asir Province, Saudi Arabia. Sixty-five of his photographs were exhibited at the First International Symposium on Islamic Architecture and Urbanism at King Faisal University in Dammam.

Ronald W. Kenyon is a member of the American-Bahraini Friendship Society and Artists of Palm Beach County.

Also by Ronald W. Kenyon

Divagations: Collected Poetry 1959-1996
Monville: Forgotten Luminary of the French Enlightenment
Monville: l'inconnu des Lumières
Le Petit Kenyon: Dining in the Environs of Paris for Walkers
Statues of Liberty: Real Stories from France
On the Trail in France
Floridians: Real Stories from the Sunshine State

Photography

Metro Portraits
Metro Messages
My Beautiful France: Landscapes
Ile-de-France, terres d'inspiration
France Images & Messages

November 20, 2016
22939

Printed in Great Britain
by Amazon